A collection of
SCOTT JOHNSTON CARTOONS

Volume 1

by
(not surprisingly)

Scott Johnston

D1501940

For information contact Scott Johnston by email at scottjcartoons@gmail.com

To Becky

With much love - thanks for all of your patience
in putting up with both my cartooning, and me

"Scott Johnston's work is insightful and very funny! A pleasure to read."

Graham Harrop, *Ten Cats*

"Scott's cartoons have universal appeal. He cracks us up with his witty and refreshing look at familiar situations. Plus, they're wicked funny!"

Dave London & **Pete Chianca**, *Pet Peeves*

"Who says cartoons can't be nice AND funny? Gentle AND witty? Simple AND layered? Scott's ideas are all over the place, yet consistently solid, and better yet, many of them are *about* something. The drawings are a hoot, but it's the writing that sticks the landing. That said, enough with the niceties - I'll never forgive him for thinking of the Chameleon With Tattoo and the Baby Waldo panels before I could. Never, Scott, NEVER."

Dave Coverly, *Speed Bump*

"I love Scott Johnston's cartoons. They always make me smile, and often laugh out loud. He's a very funny guy."

Kevin Fagan, *Drabble*

"Scott has a unique way of looking at life. Taking what can be an ordinary subject, giving it a twist and coming up with something really funny."

Adrian Raeside, *The Other Coast*

"Ages from now a very learned comic scholar in the distant future will stumble across this volume and shout '*Eureka!... 'Tis the holy grail of early 21st century Canadian cartoon collections!*'
It will then undoubtedly be snapped up at auction by an evil, comic-art-hoarding-mega-trillionaire and never be seen again.
The moral of the story?... Keep your copy of Scott's cartoon book in a safe. Your great, great, great, great, great, great grandchildren will be forever grateful."

Leigh Rubin, *Rubes*®

"Scott has a gentle wit that is very funny. His cartoons bring a smile and a chuckle every time!"

Sandra Bell-Lundy, *Between Friends*

PREFACE

Like most cartoonists, I grew up scribbling, and would spend hours drawing popular cartoon characters, creating my own, and cutting favourite comic strips out of the newspaper.

Inevitably, over the years my time devoted to cartooning gave way to increasing amounts of work at school and university, and then at a job that while less fun than cartooning, at least paid the bills.

I continued to scribble in my free time, and have been fortunate to draw an editorial cartoon for *The Auroran* newspaper since October 2000. This in turn lead to my being accepted into the Association of Canadian Cartoonists.

When I finally retired from my "real" job, and with time on my hands, I returned to the drawing board. While editorial cartoons presented their own creative challenges and rewards, I soon discovered that the freedom to draw whatever I wanted in my own single panel gag cartoons was a lot more fun.

This book includes some of my more popular ones, as well as some personal favourites.
I hope you enjoy them as much as I did drawing them.

Scott Johnston

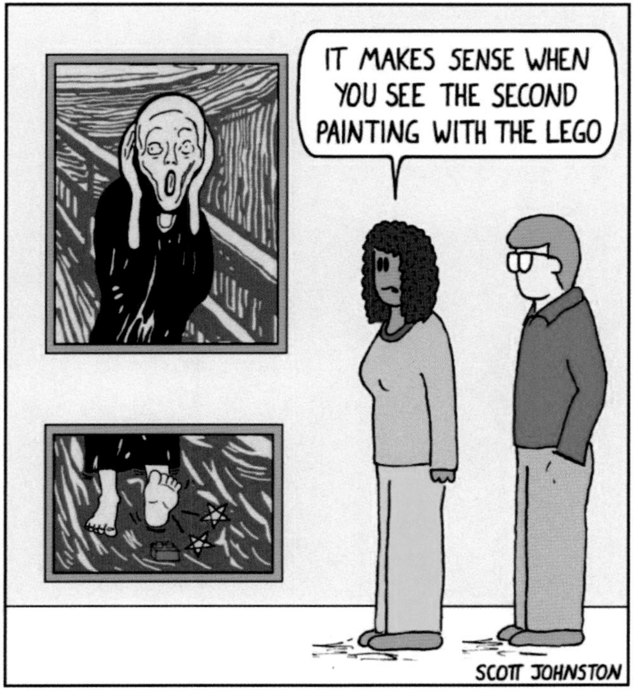
IT MAKES SENSE WHEN YOU SEE THE SECOND PAINTING WITH THE LEGO
SCOTT JOHNSTON

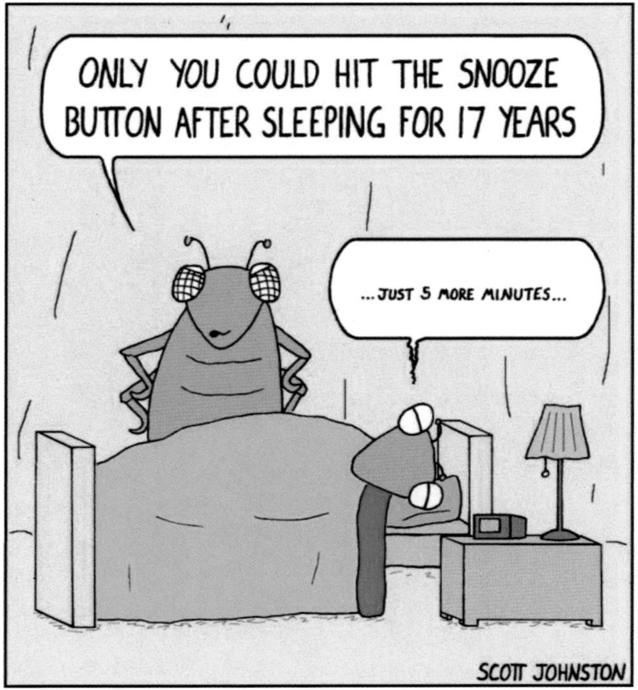
ONLY YOU COULD HIT THE SNOOZE BUTTON AFTER SLEEPING FOR 17 YEARS
...JUST 5 MORE MINUTES...
SCOTT JOHNSTON

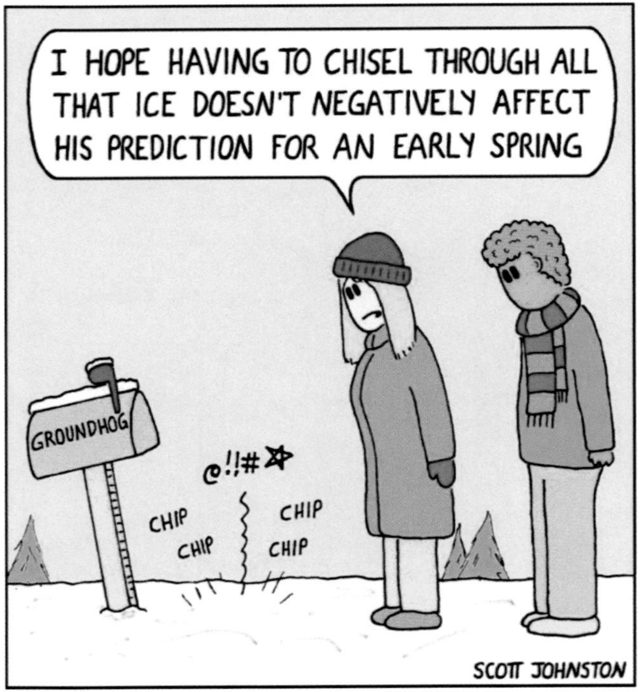
I HOPE HAVING TO CHISEL THROUGH ALL THAT ICE DOESN'T NEGATIVELY AFFECT HIS PREDICTION FOR AN EARLY SPRING
GROUNDHOG
@!!#
CHIP
CHIP
CHIP
CHIP
SCOTT JOHNSTON

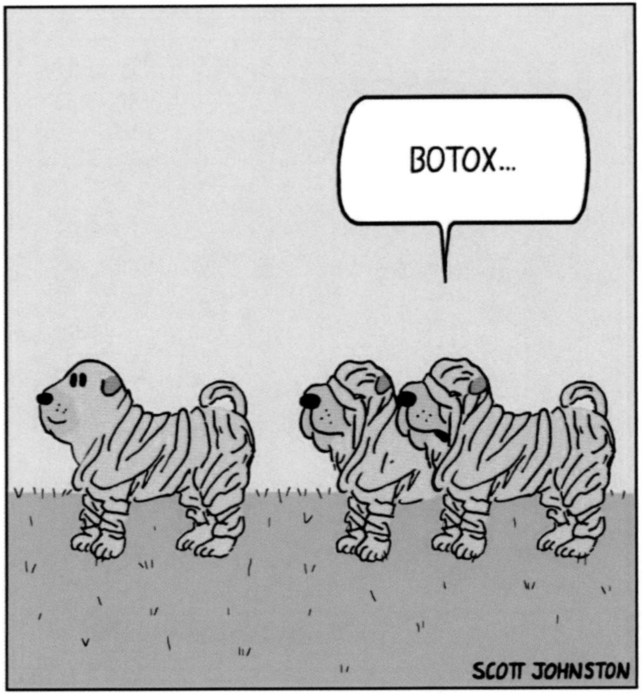
BOTOX...
SCOTT JOHNSTON

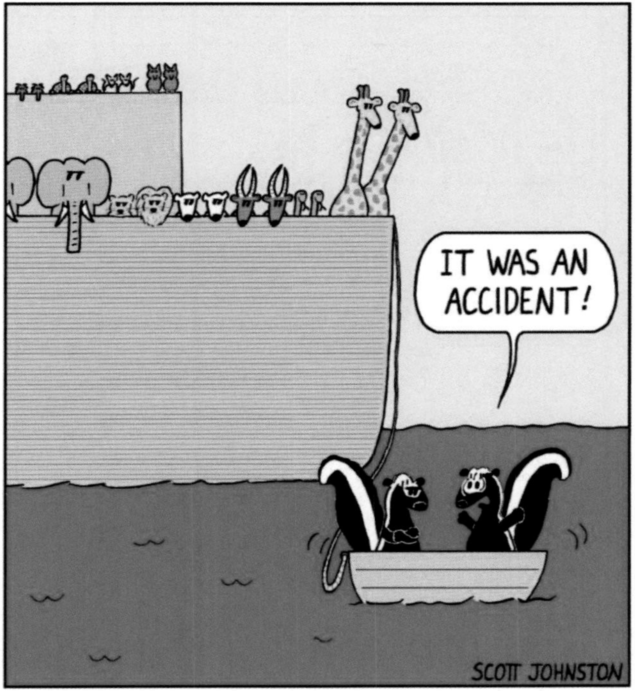
IT WAS AN ACCIDENT!
SCOTT JOHNSTON

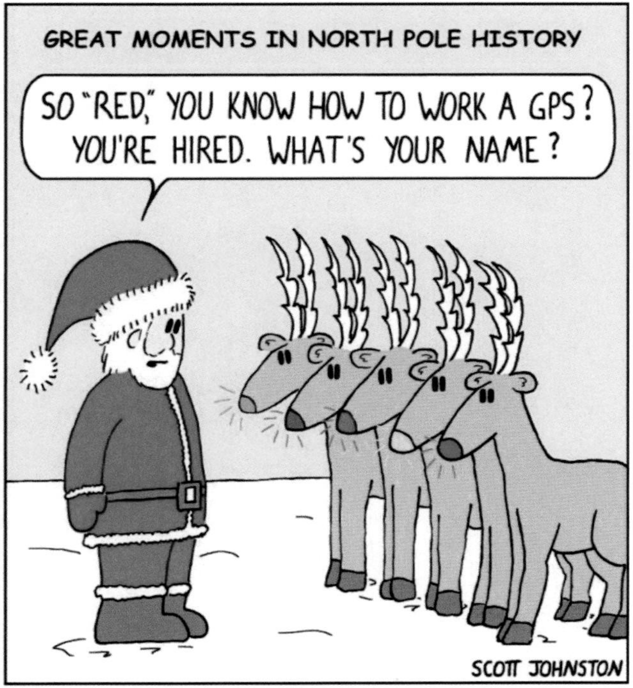
GREAT MOMENTS IN NORTH POLE HISTORY
SO "RED," YOU KNOW HOW TO WORK A GPS? YOU'RE HIRED. WHAT'S YOUR NAME?
SCOTT JOHNSTON

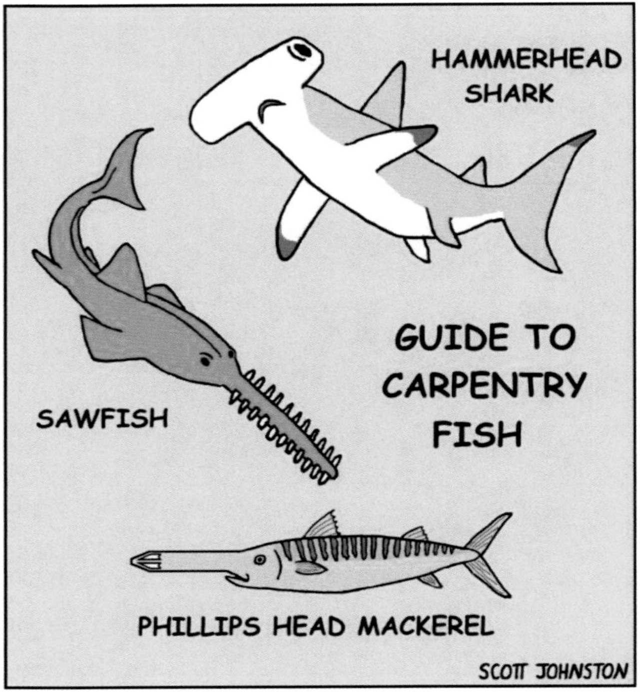
HAMMERHEAD SHARK
SAWFISH
GUIDE TO CARPENTRY FISH
PHILLIPS HEAD MACKEREL
SCOTT JOHNSTON

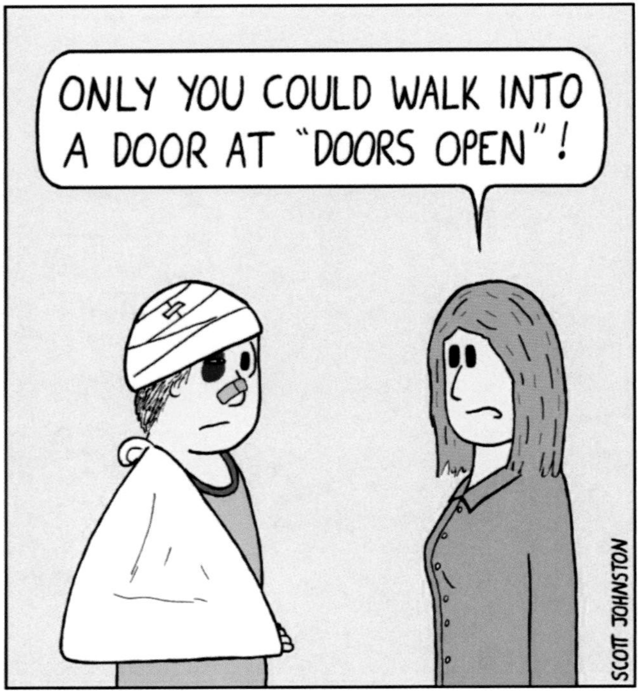
ONLY YOU COULD WALK INTO A DOOR AT "DOORS OPEN"!
SCOTT JOHNSTON

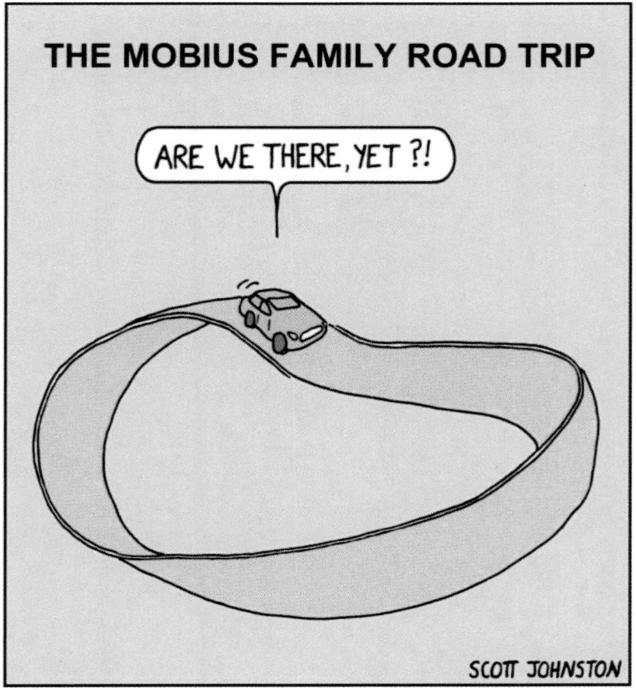
THE MOBIUS FAMILY ROAD TRIP
ARE WE THERE, YET ?!
SCOTT JOHNSTON

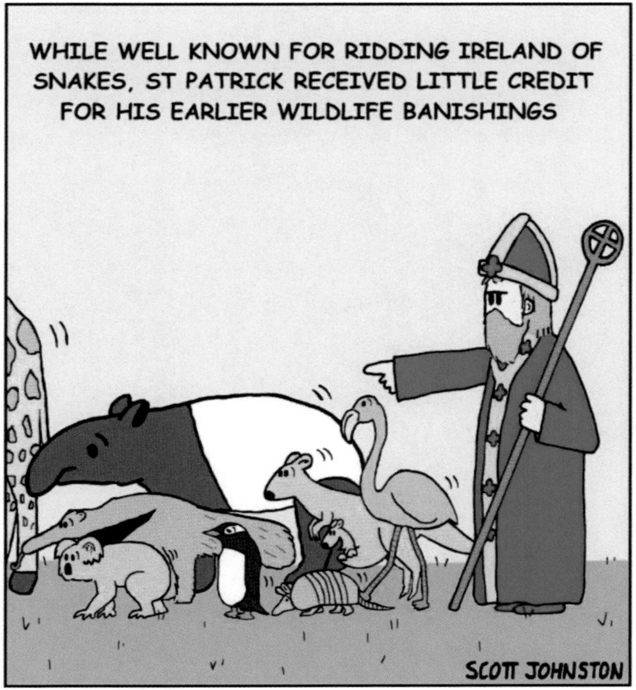
WHILE WELL KNOWN FOR RIDDING IRELAND OF SNAKES, ST PATRICK RECEIVED LITTLE CREDIT FOR HIS EARLIER WILDLIFE BANISHINGS
SCOTT JOHNSTON

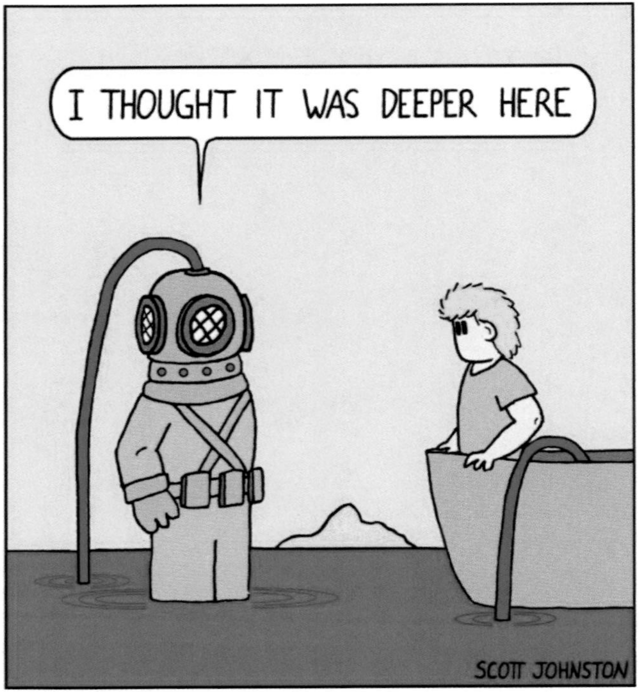
I THOUGHT IT WAS DEEPER HERE
SCOTT JOHNSTON

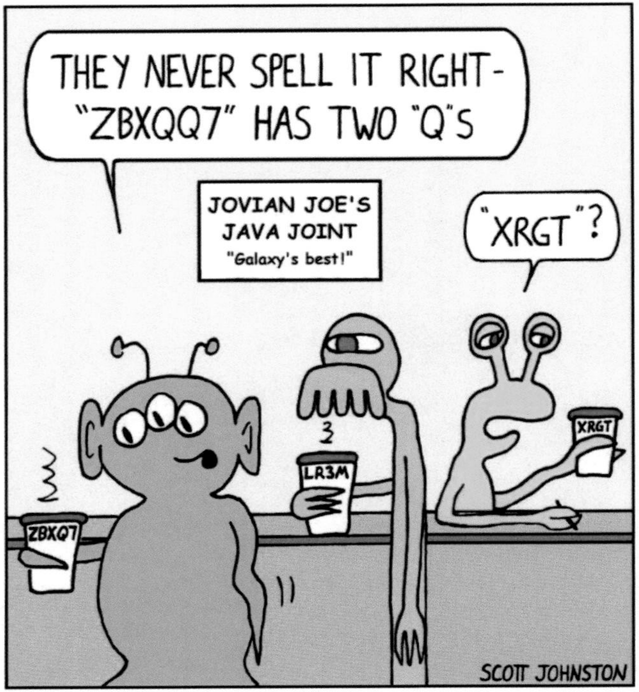
THEY NEVER SPELL IT RIGHT-
"ZBXQQ7" HAS TWO "Q"S
JOVIAN JOE'S
JAVA JOINT
"Galaxy's best!"
"XRGT"?
ZBXQ7
LR3M
XRGT
SCOTT JOHNSTON

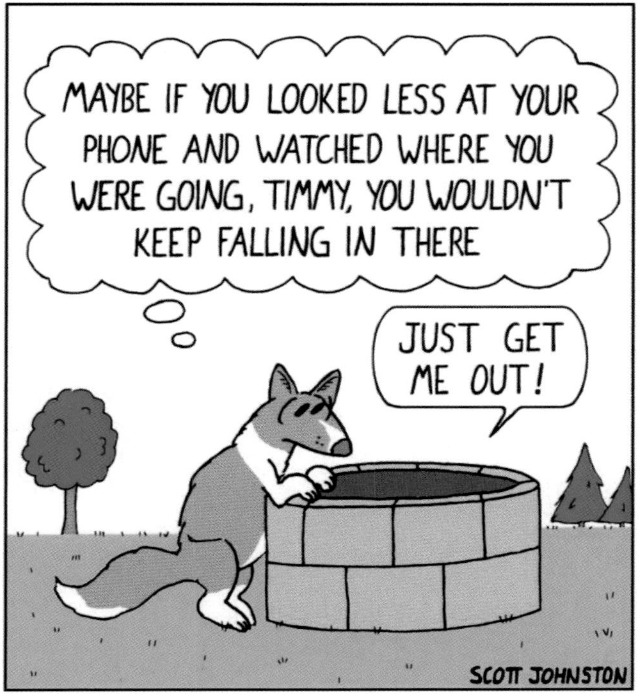
MAYBE IF YOU LOOKED LESS AT YOUR PHONE AND WATCHED WHERE YOU WERE GOING, TIMMY, YOU WOULDN'T KEEP FALLING IN THERE
JUST GET ME OUT!
SCOTT JOHNSTON

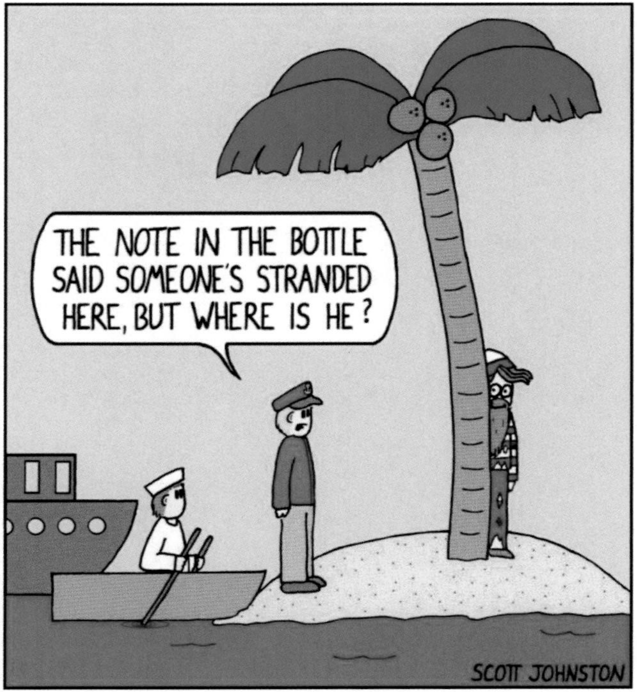
THE NOTE IN THE BOTTLE SAID SOMEONE'S STRANDED HERE, BUT WHERE IS HE?
SCOTT JOHNSTON

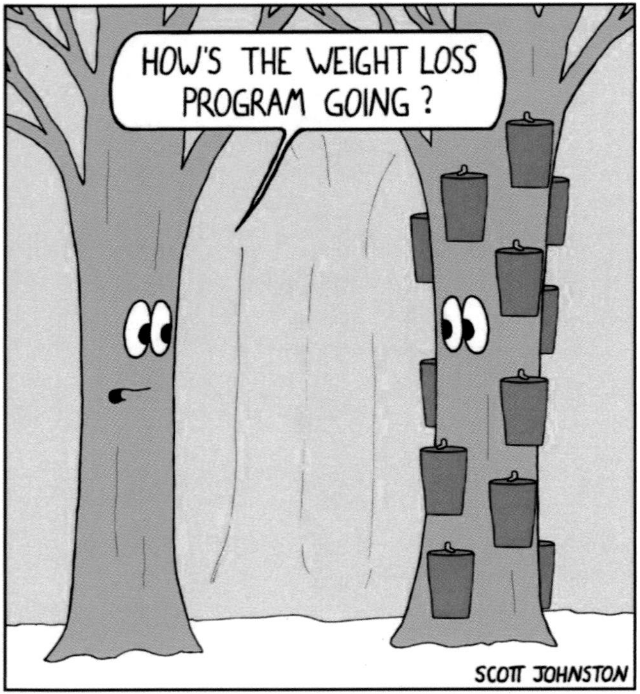
HOW'S THE WEIGHT LOSS PROGRAM GOING ?
SCOTT JOHNSTON

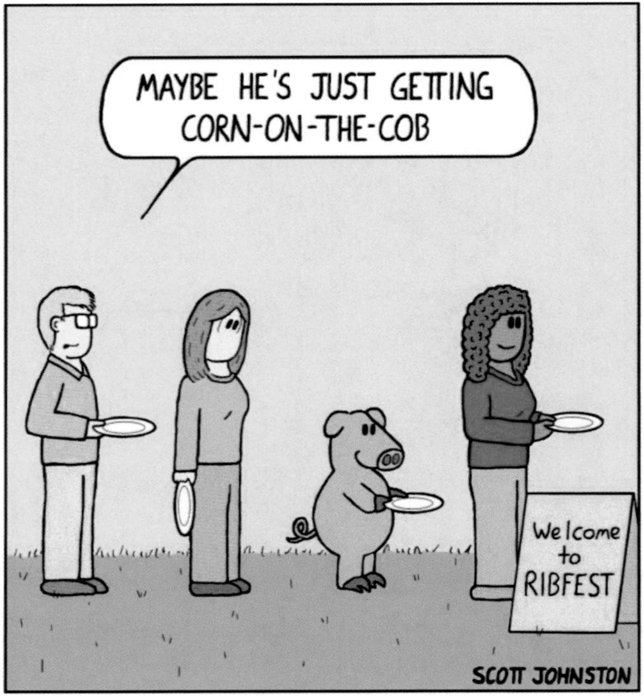
MAYBE HE'S JUST GETTING CORN-ON-THE-COB
Welcome to RIBFEST
SCOTT JOHNSTON

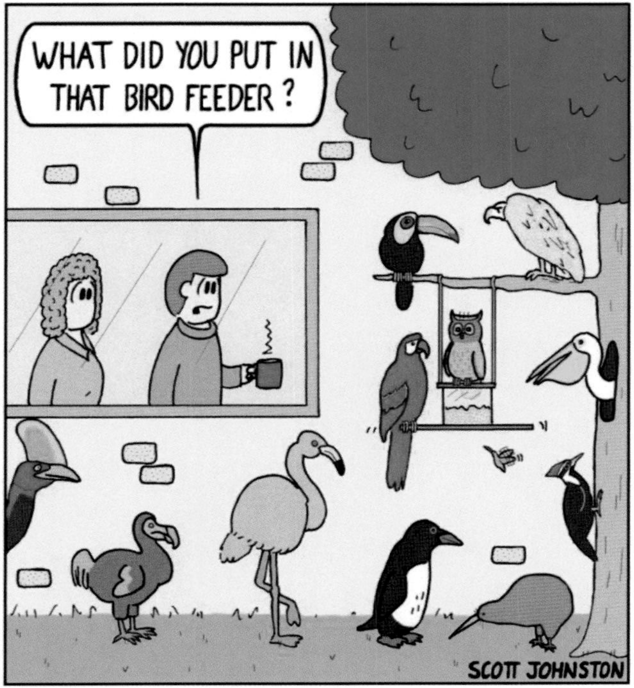
WHAT DID YOU PUT IN THAT BIRD FEEDER?
SCOTT JOHNSTON

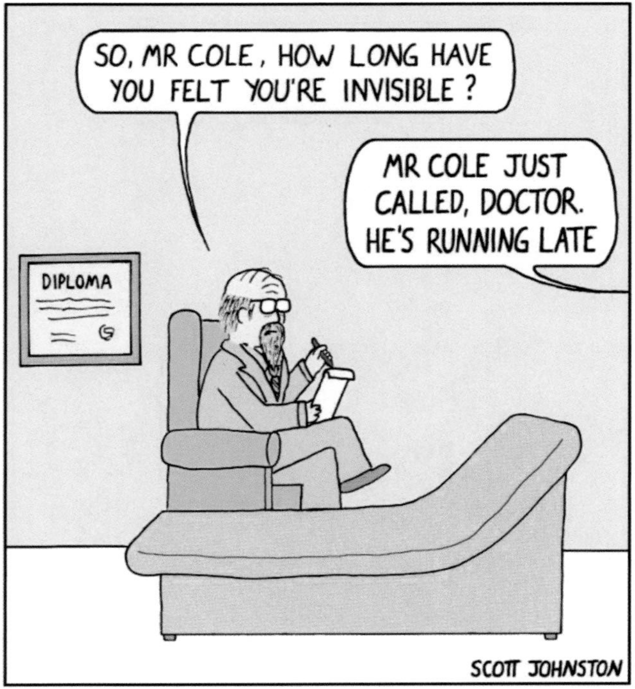
SO, MR COLE, HOW LONG HAVE YOU FELT YOU'RE INVISIBLE?
MR COLE JUST CALLED, DOCTOR. HE'S RUNNING LATE
DIPLOMA
SCOTT JOHNSTON

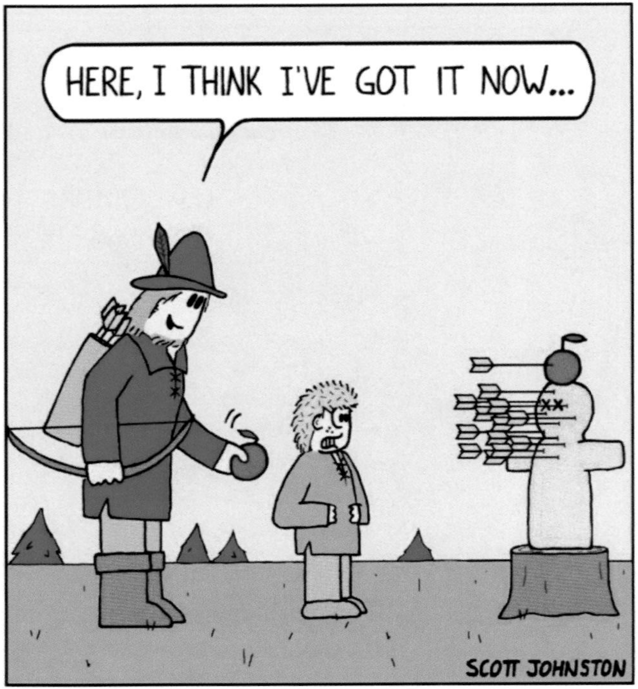
HERE, I THINK I'VE GOT IT NOW...
SCOTT JOHNSTON

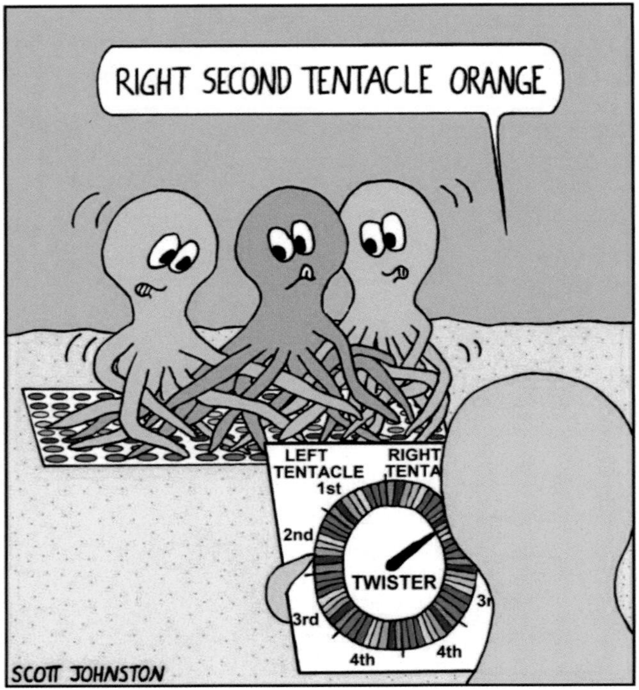
RIGHT SECOND TENTACLE ORANGE
LEFT TENTACLE
RIGHT TENTA
1st
2nd
3rd
4th
4th
TWISTER
SCOTT JOHNSTON

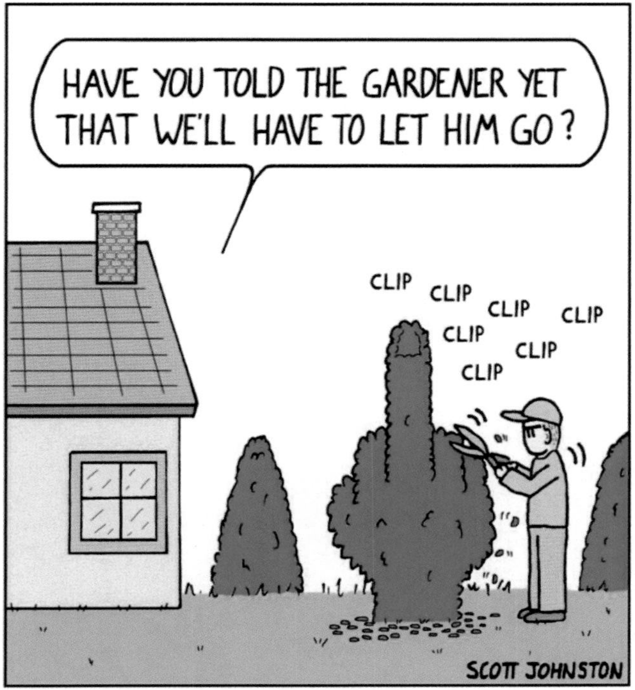
HAVE YOU TOLD THE GARDENER YET THAT WE'LL HAVE TO LET HIM GO?
CLIP CLIP CLIP CLIP CLIP CLIP CLIP
SCOTT JOHNSTON

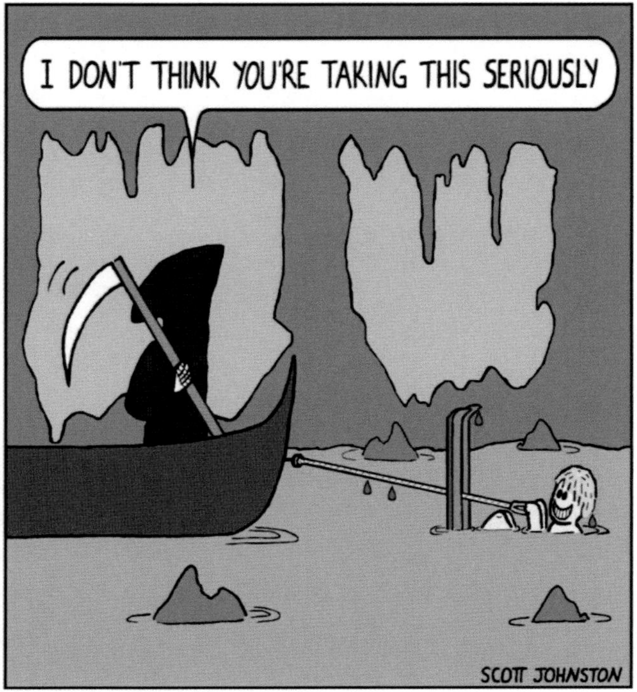
I DON'T THINK YOU'RE TAKING THIS SERIOUSLY
SCOTT JOHNSTON

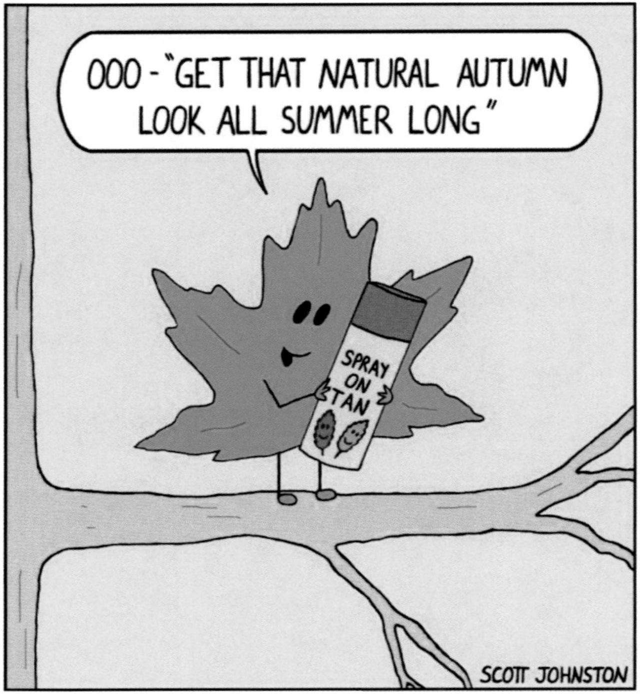
OOO - "GET THAT NATURAL AUTUMN LOOK ALL SUMMER LONG"
SPRAY ON TAN
SCOTT JOHNSTON

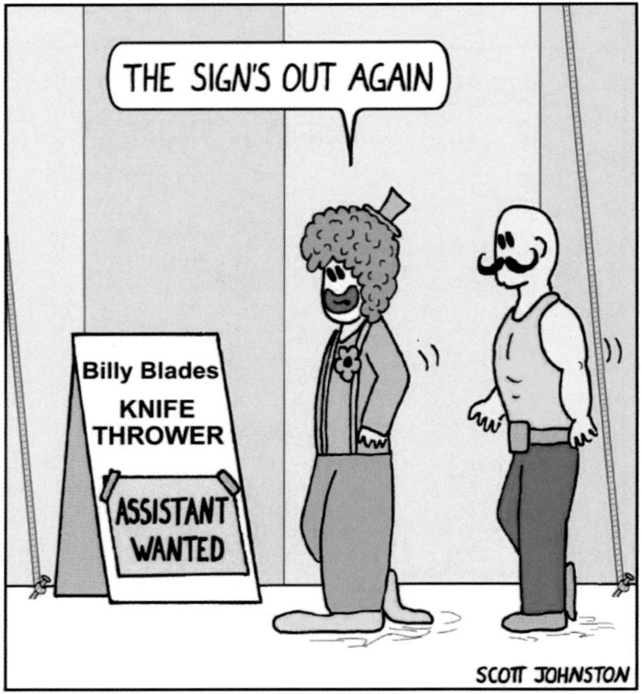
THE SIGN'S OUT AGAIN
Billy Blades
KNIFE THROWER
ASSISTANT WANTED
SCOTT JOHNSTON

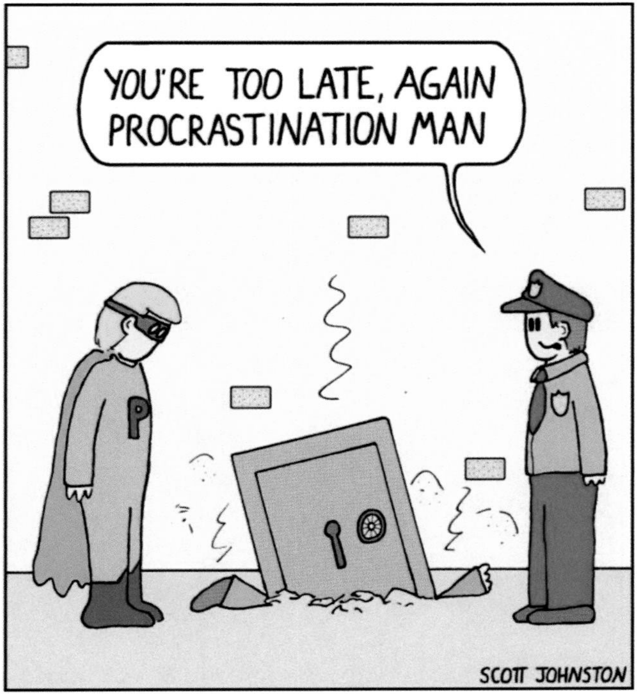
YOU'RE TOO LATE, AGAIN PROCRASTINATION MAN
P
SCOTT JOHNSTON

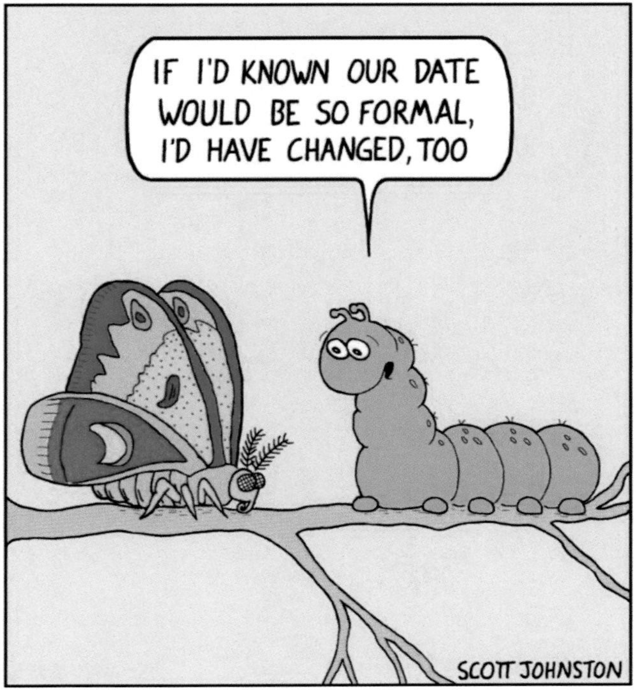
IF I'D KNOWN OUR DATE WOULD BE SO FORMAL, I'D HAVE CHANGED, TOO
SCOTT JOHNSTON

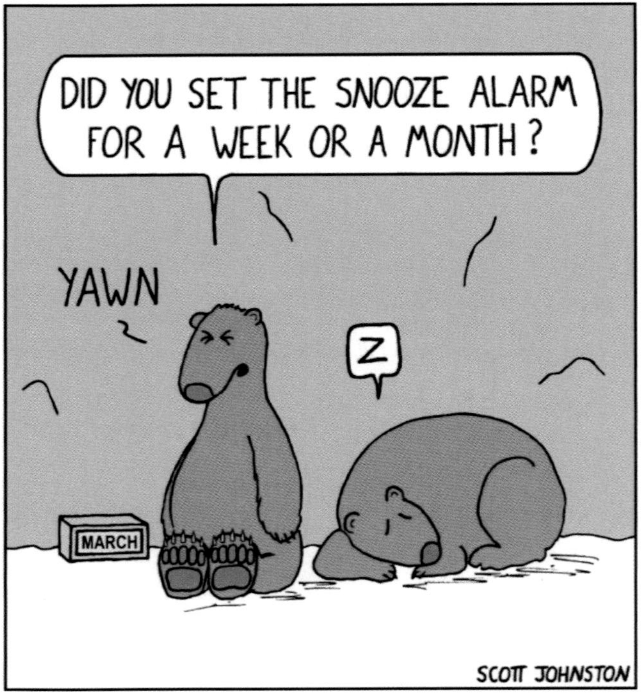
DID YOU SET THE SNOOZE ALARM FOR A WEEK OR A MONTH?
YAWN
Z
MARCH
SCOTT JOHNSTON

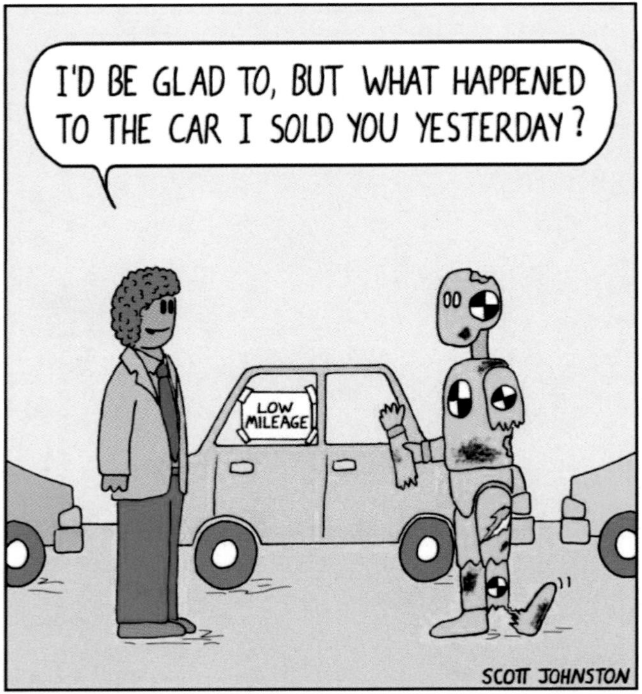
I'D BE GLAD TO, BUT WHAT HAPPENED TO THE CAR I SOLD YOU YESTERDAY?
LOW MILEAGE
SCOTT JOHNSTON

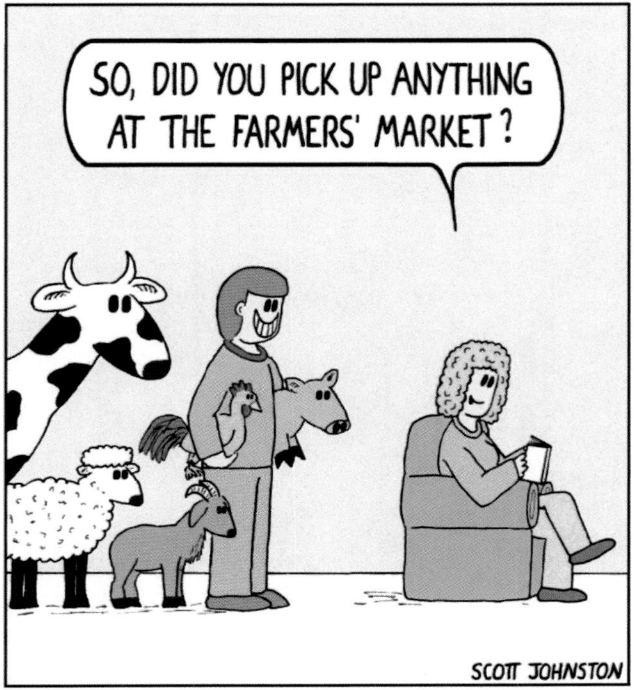

SO, DID YOU PICK UP ANYTHING AT THE FARMERS' MARKET?
SCOTT JOHNSTON

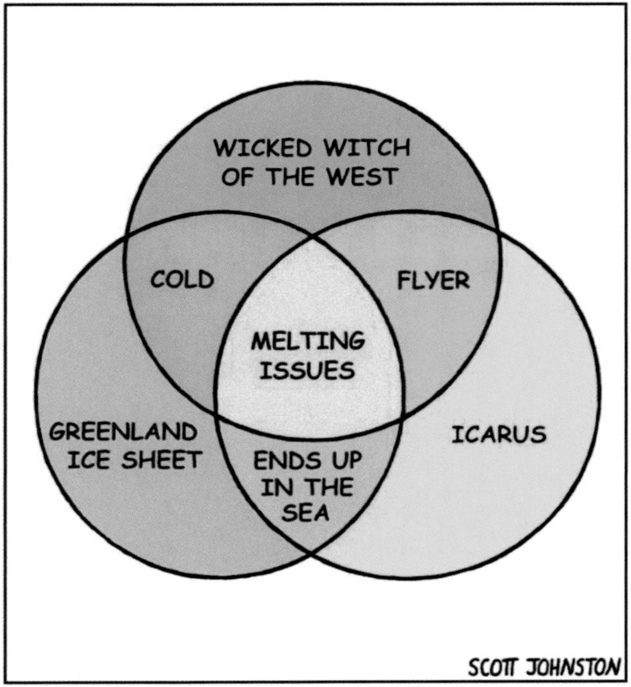

WICKED WITCH OF THE WEST
COLD
FLYER
MELTING ISSUES
GREENLAND ICE SHEET
ENDS UP IN THE SEA
ICARUS
SCOTT JOHNSTON

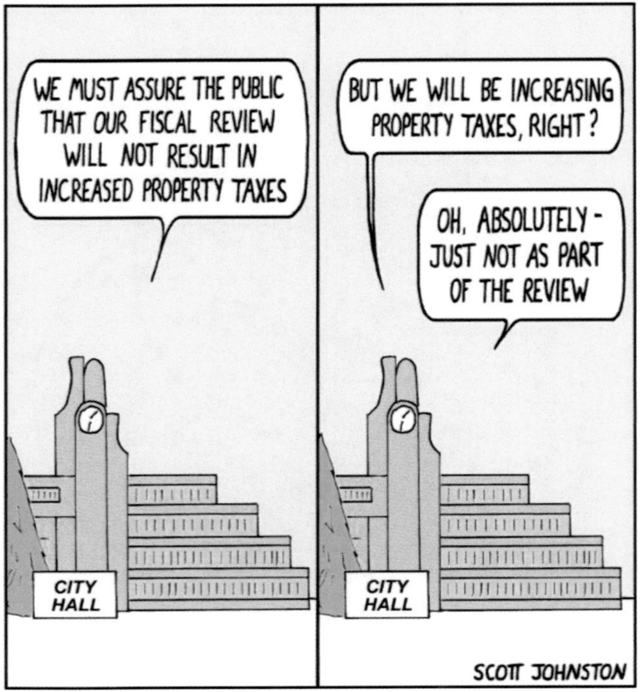
WE MUST ASSURE THE PUBLIC THAT OUR FISCAL REVIEW WILL NOT RESULT IN INCREASED PROPERTY TAXES
CITY HALL
BUT WE WILL BE INCREASING PROPERTY TAXES, RIGHT?
OH, ABSOLUTELY - JUST NOT AS PART OF THE REVIEW
CITY HALL
SCOTT JOHNSTON

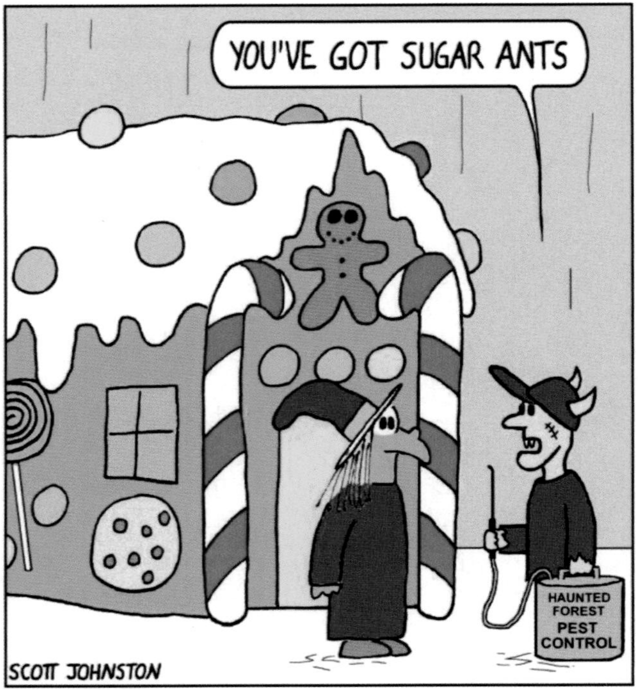
YOU'VE GOT SUGAR ANTS
HAUNTED FOREST PEST CONTROL
SCOTT JOHNSTON

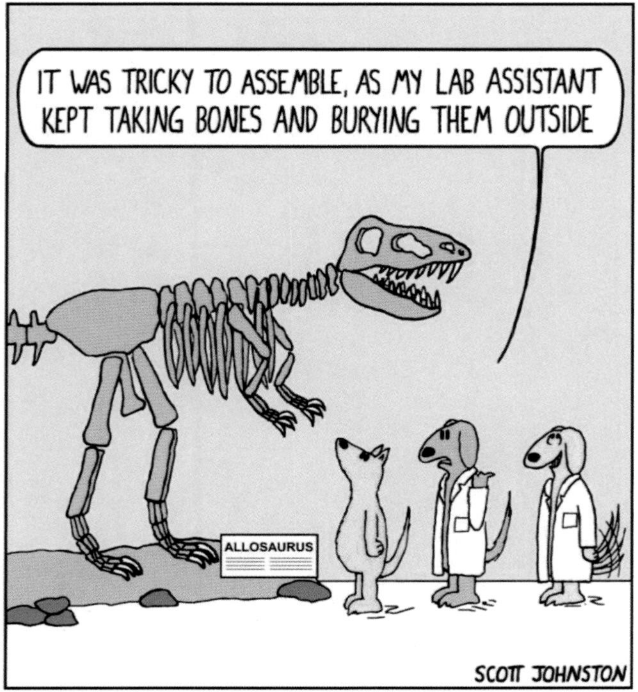
IT WAS TRICKY TO ASSEMBLE, AS MY LAB ASSISTANT KEPT TAKING BONES AND BURYING THEM OUTSIDE
ALLOSAURUS
SCOTT JOHNSTON

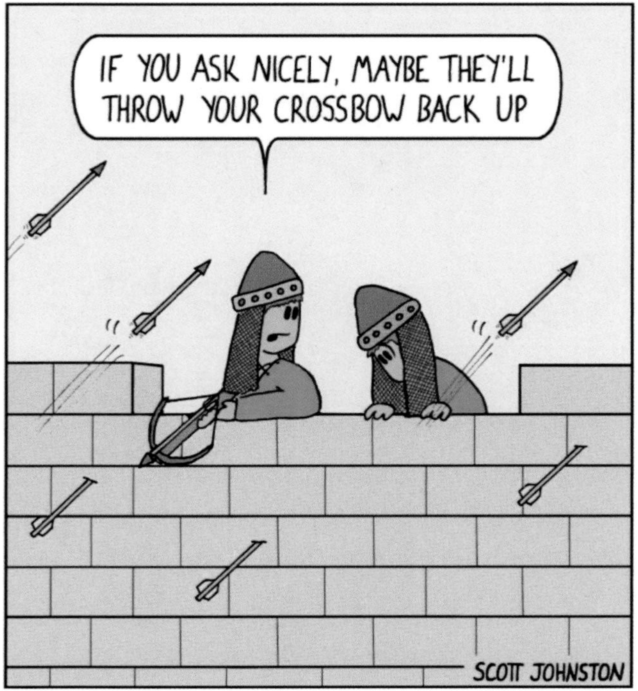
IF YOU ASK NICELY, MAYBE THEY'LL THROW YOUR CROSSBOW BACK UP
SCOTT JOHNSTON

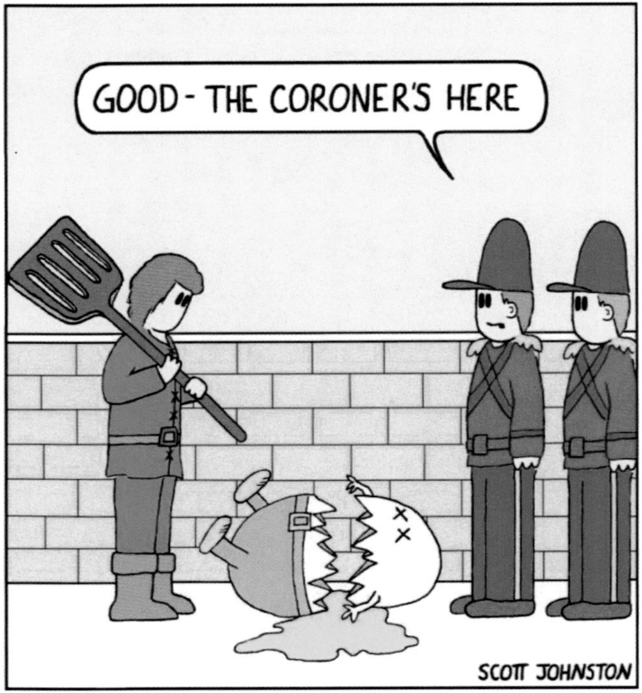
GOOD - THE CORONER'S HERE
SCOTT JOHNSTON

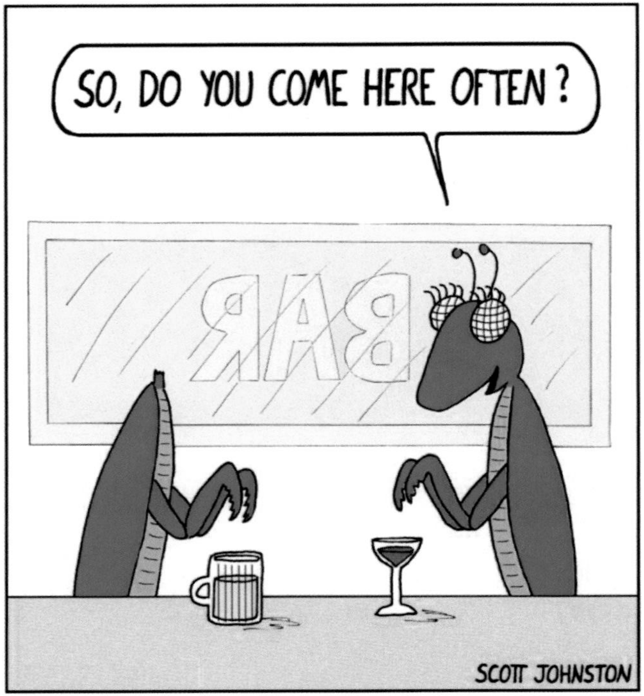
SO, DO YOU COME HERE OFTEN ?
BAR
SCOTT JOHNSTON

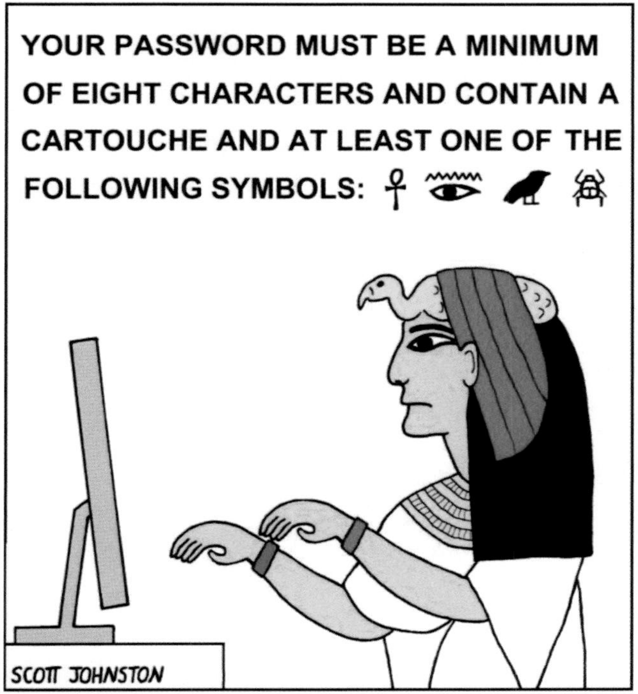
YOUR PASSWORD MUST BE A MINIMUM OF EIGHT CHARACTERS AND CONTAIN A CARTOUCHE AND AT LEAST ONE OF THE FOLLOWING SYMBOLS:
SCOTT JOHNSTON

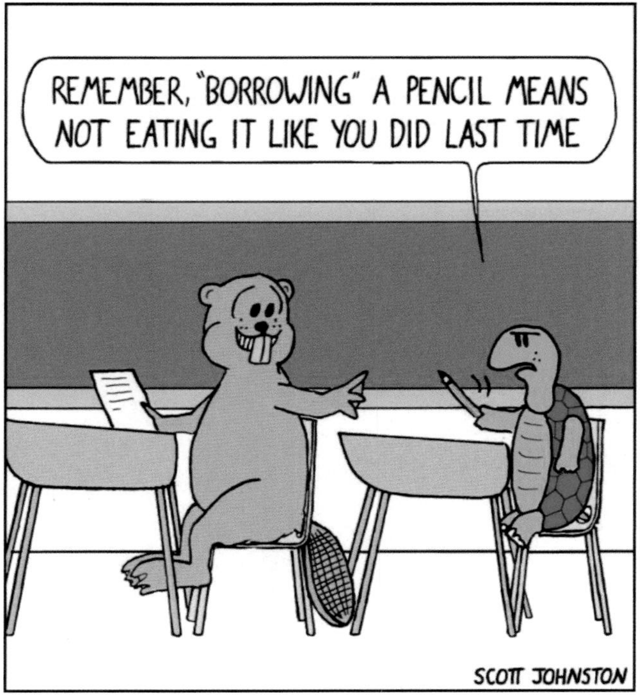
REMEMBER, "BORROWING" A PENCIL MEANS NOT EATING IT LIKE YOU DID LAST TIME
SCOTT JOHNSTON

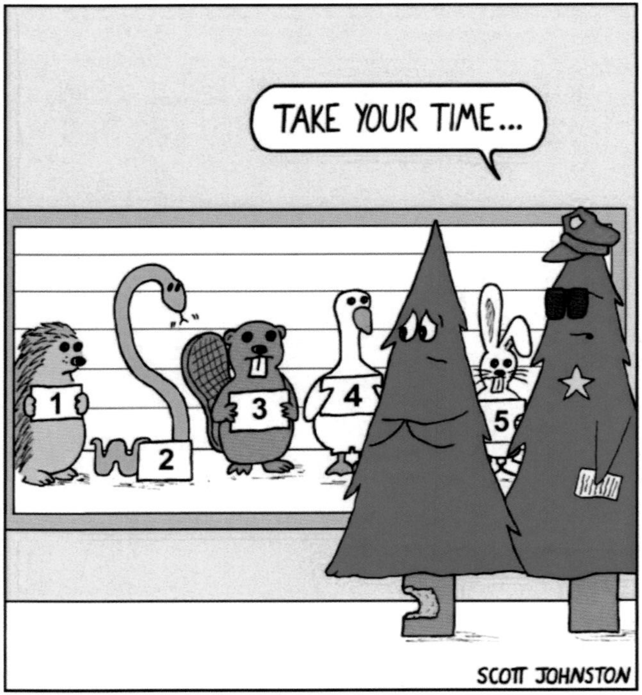
TAKE YOUR TIME...
1
2
3
4
5
SCOTT JOHNSTON

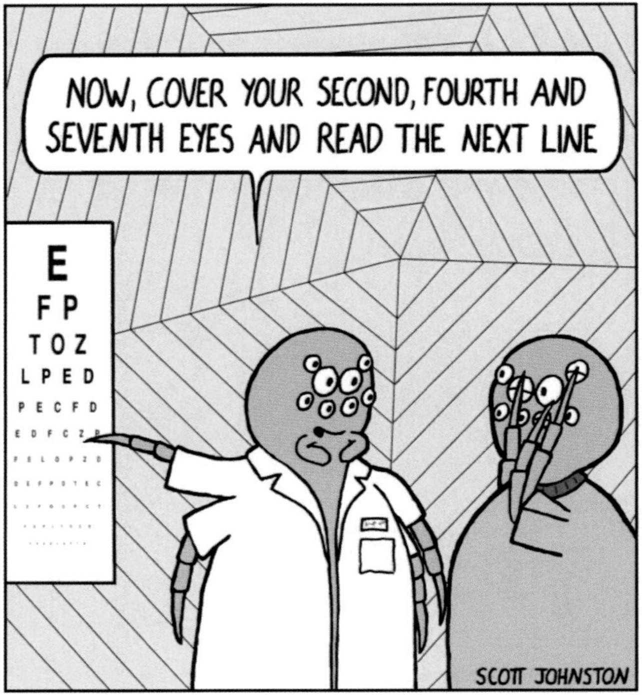
NOW, COVER YOUR SECOND, FOURTH AND SEVENTH EYES AND READ THE NEXT LINE
E
F P
T O Z
L P E D
P E C F D
SCOTT JOHNSTON

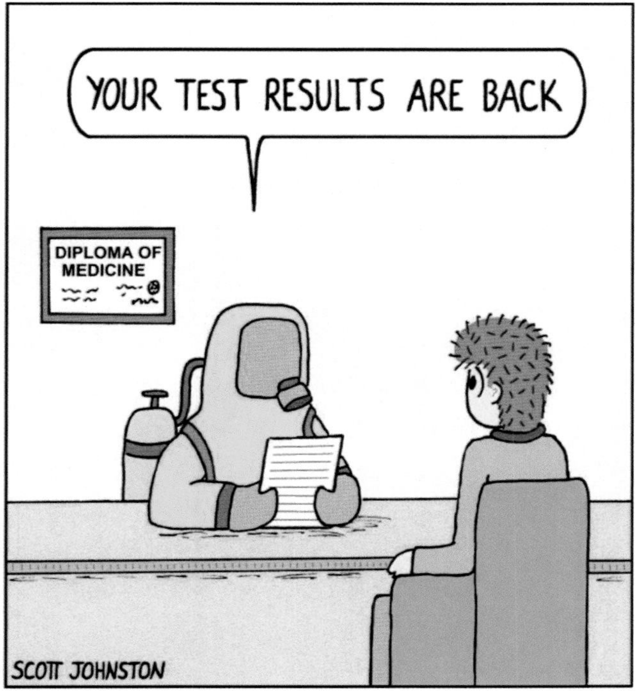
YOUR TEST RESULTS ARE BACK
DIPLOMA OF MEDICINE
SCOTT JOHNSTON

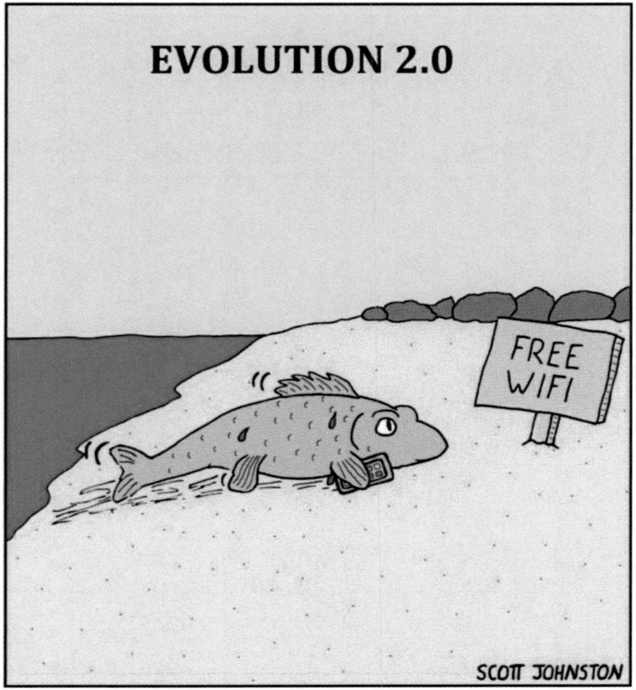
EVOLUTION 2.0
FREE WIFI
SCOTT JOHNSTON

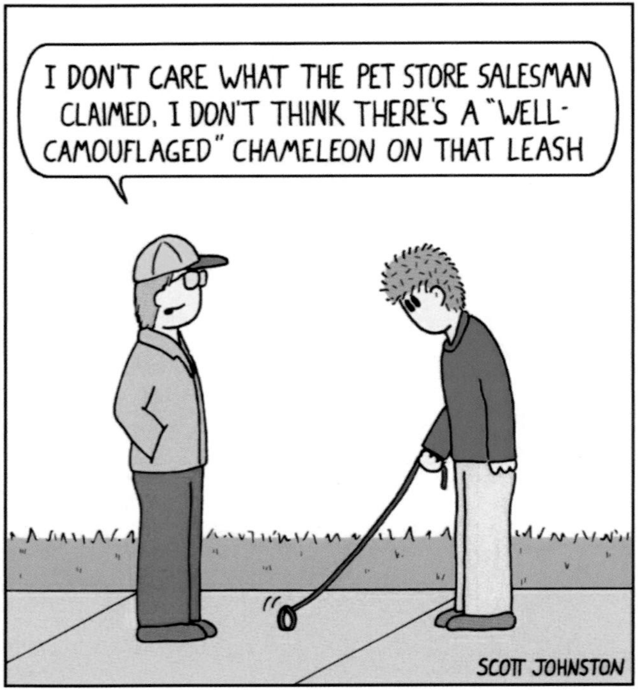
I DON'T CARE WHAT THE PET STORE SALESMAN CLAIMED. I DON'T THINK THERE'S A "WELL-CAMOUFLAGED" CHAMELEON ON THAT LEASH
SCOTT JOHNSTON

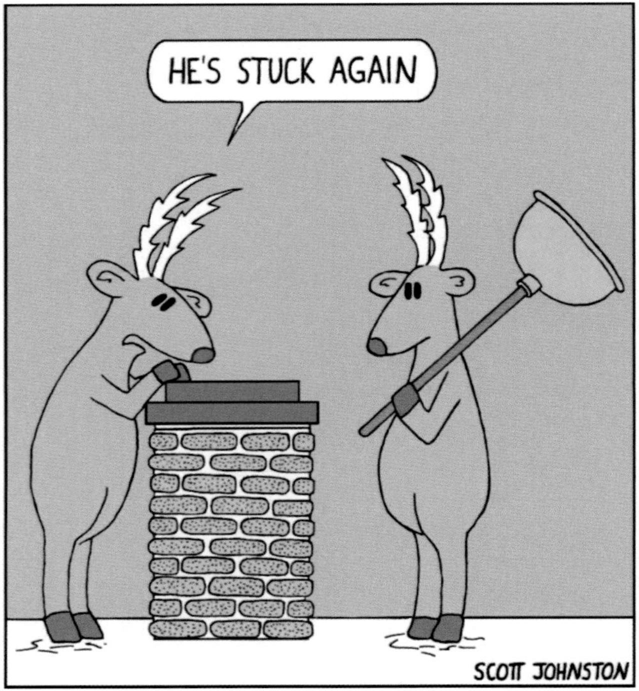
HE'S STUCK AGAIN
SCOTT JOHNSTON

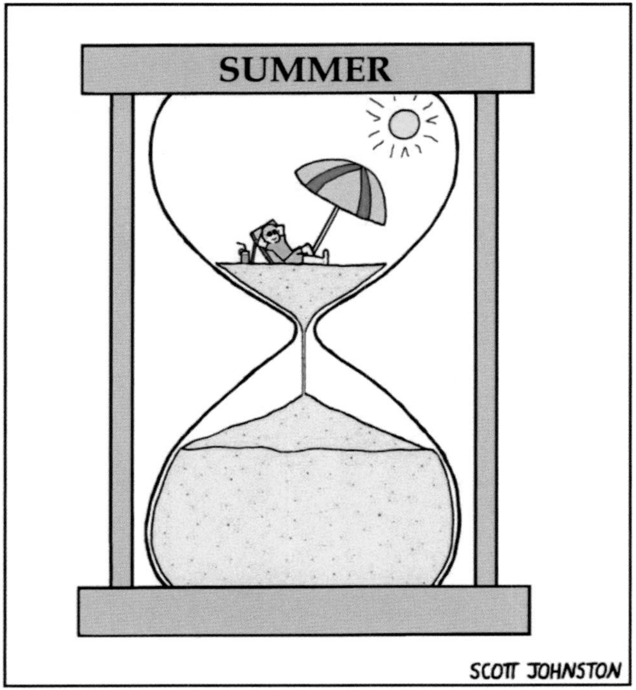
SUMMER
SCOTT JOHNSTON

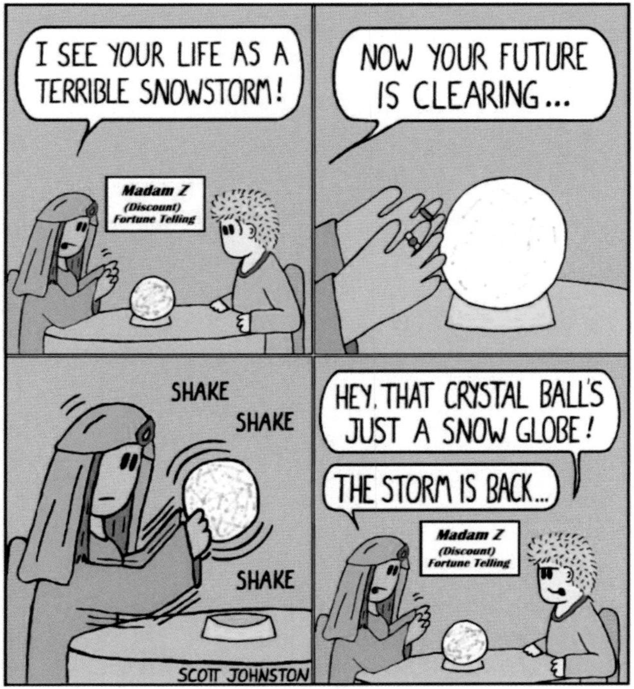
I SEE YOUR LIFE AS A TERRIBLE SNOWSTORM!
Madam Z (Discount) Fortune Telling
NOW YOUR FUTURE IS CLEARING...
SHAKE
SHAKE
SHAKE
SCOTT JOHNSTON
HEY, THAT CRYSTAL BALL'S JUST A SNOW GLOBE!
THE STORM IS BACK...
Madam Z (Discount) Fortune Telling

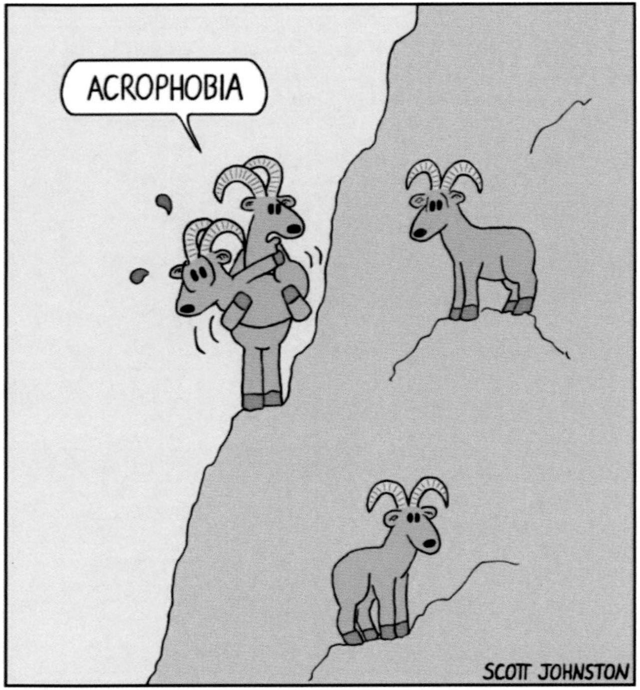
ACROPHOBIA
SCOTT JOHNSTON

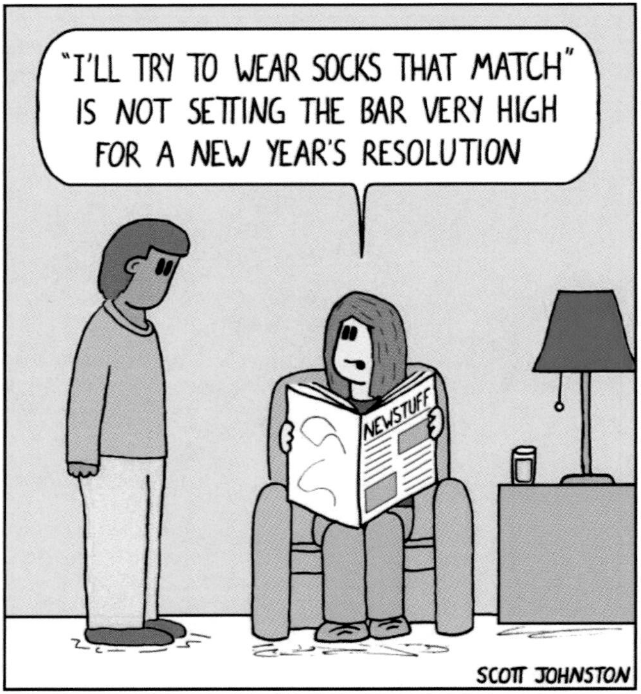
"I'LL TRY TO WEAR SOCKS THAT MATCH" IS NOT SETTING THE BAR VERY HIGH FOR A NEW YEAR'S RESOLUTION
NEWSTUFF
SCOTT JOHNSTON

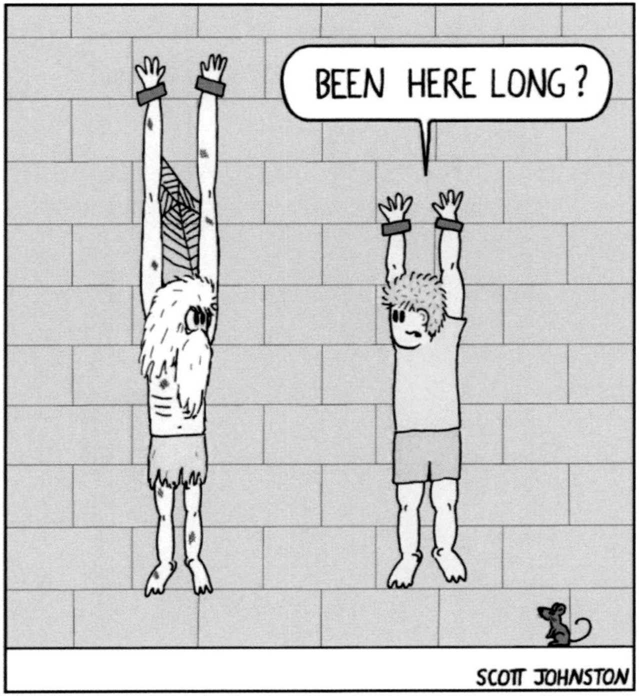
BEEN HERE LONG?
SCOTT JOHNSTON

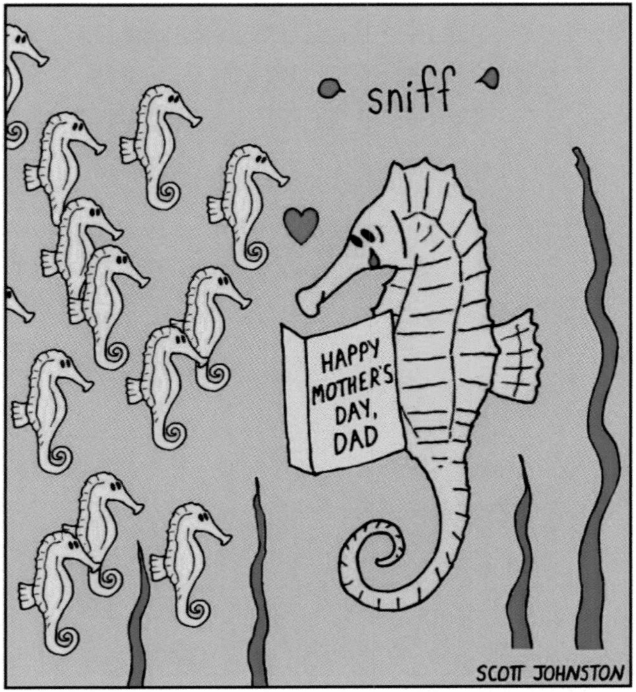
sniff
HAPPY MOTHER'S DAY, DAD
SCOTT JOHNSTON

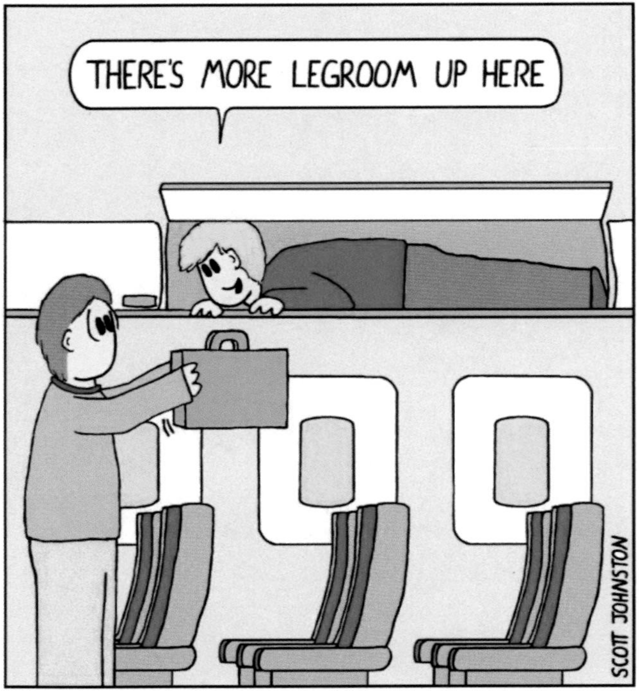
THERE'S MORE LEGROOM UP HERE
SCOTT JOHNSTON

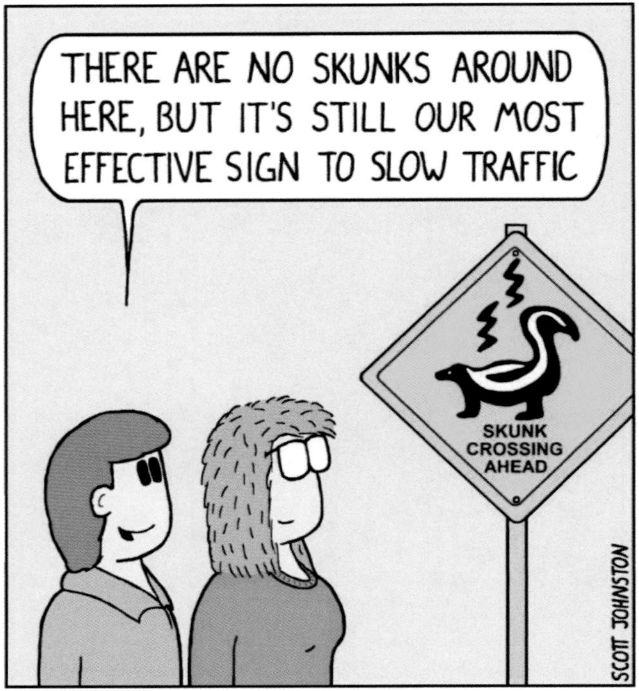
THERE ARE NO SKUNKS AROUND HERE, BUT IT'S STILL OUR MOST EFFECTIVE SIGN TO SLOW TRAFFIC
SKUNK CROSSING AHEAD
SCOTT JOHNSTON

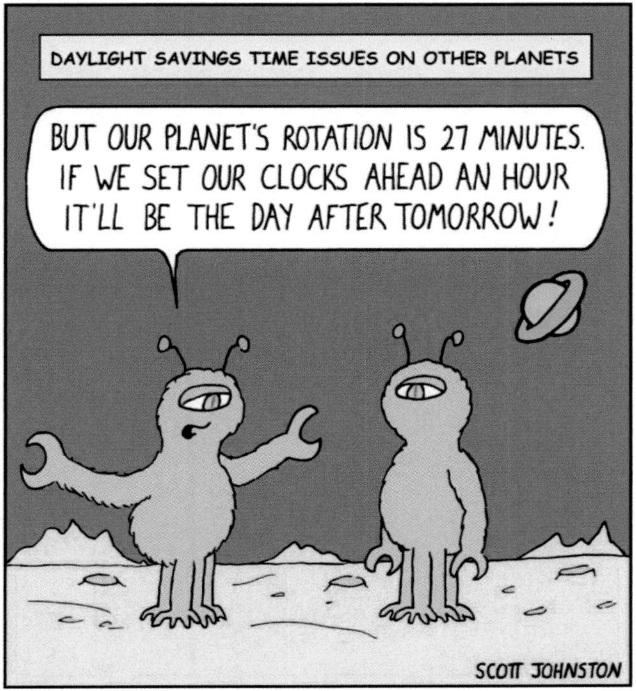
DAYLIGHT SAVINGS TIME ISSUES ON OTHER PLANETS
BUT OUR PLANET'S ROTATION IS 27 MINUTES. IF WE SET OUR CLOCKS AHEAD AN HOUR IT'LL BE THE DAY AFTER TOMORROW!
SCOTT JOHNSTON

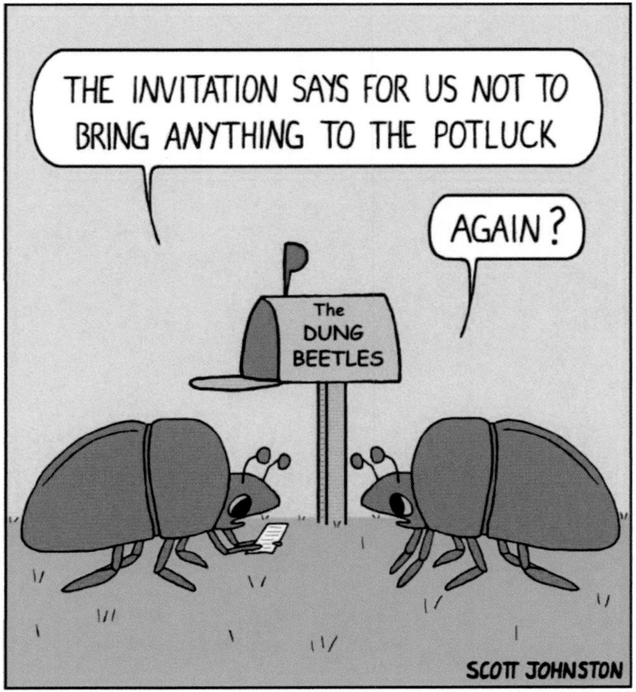
THE INVITATION SAYS FOR US NOT TO BRING ANYTHING TO THE POTLUCK
AGAIN?
The DUNG BEETLES
SCOTT JOHNSTON

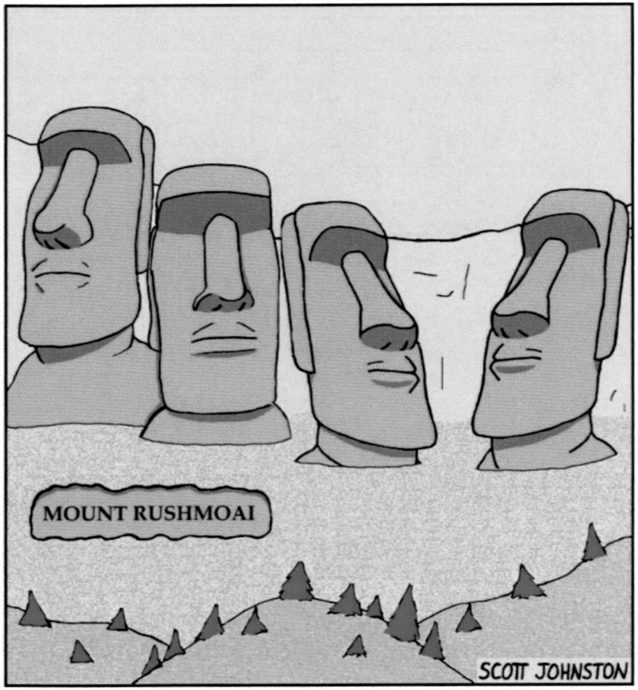
MOUNT RUSHMOAI
SCOTT JOHNSTON

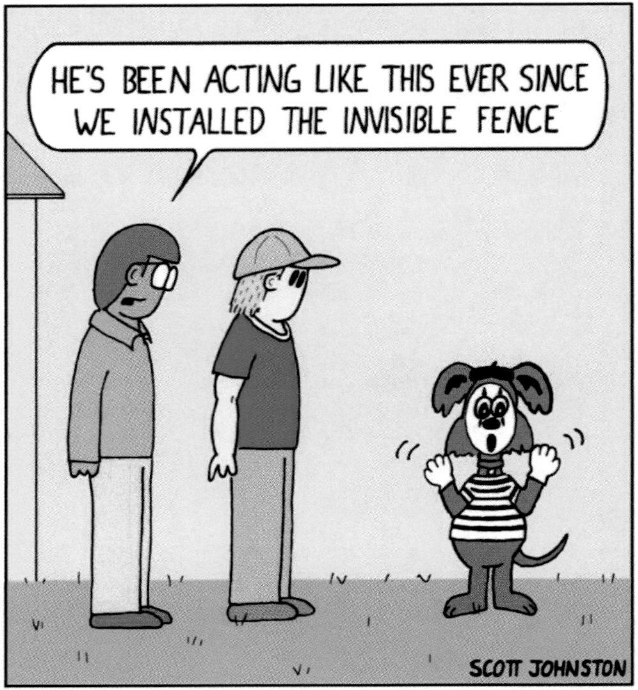
HE'S BEEN ACTING LIKE THIS EVER SINCE WE INSTALLED THE INVISIBLE FENCE
SCOTT JOHNSTON

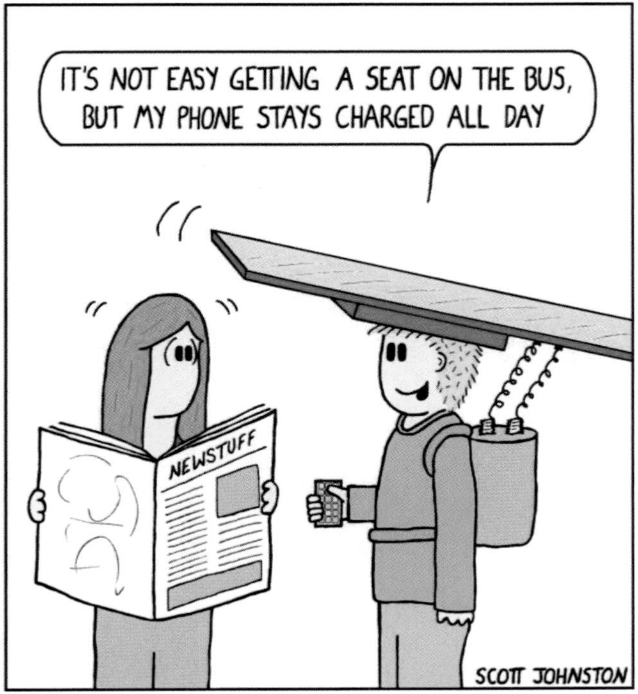
IT'S NOT EASY GETTING A SEAT ON THE BUS, BUT MY PHONE STAYS CHARGED ALL DAY
NEWSTUFF
SCOTT JOHNSTON

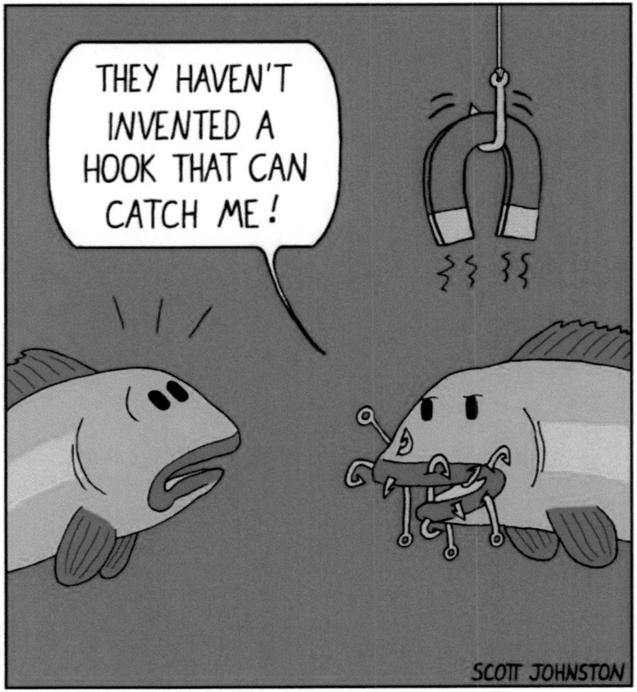
THEY HAVEN'T INVENTED A HOOK THAT CAN CATCH ME!
SCOTT JOHNSTON

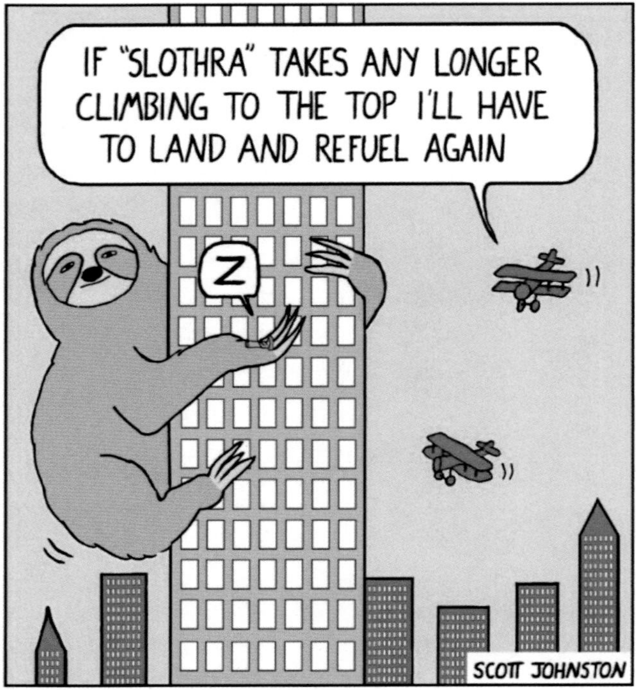
IF "SLOTHRA" TAKES ANY LONGER CLIMBING TO THE TOP I'LL HAVE TO LAND AND REFUEL AGAIN
Z
SCOTT JOHNSTON

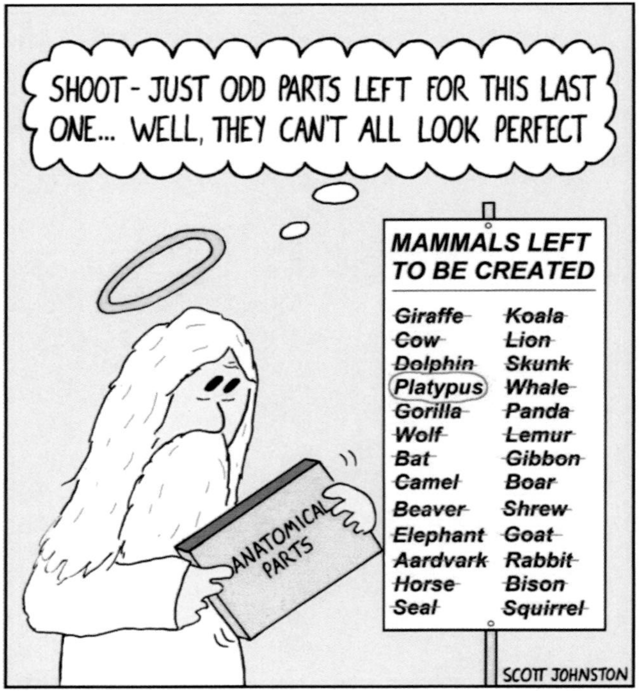
SHOOT - JUST ODD PARTS LEFT FOR THIS LAST ONE... WELL, THEY CAN'T ALL LOOK PERFECT
MAMMALS LEFT TO BE CREATED
Giraffe
Cow
Dolphin
Platypus
Gorilla
Wolf
Bat
Camel
Beaver
Elephant
Aardvark
Horse
Seal
Koala
Lion
Skunk
Whale
Panda
Lemur
Gibbon
Boar
Shrew
Goat
Rabbit
Bison
Squirrel
ANATOMICAL PARTS
SCOTT JOHNSTON

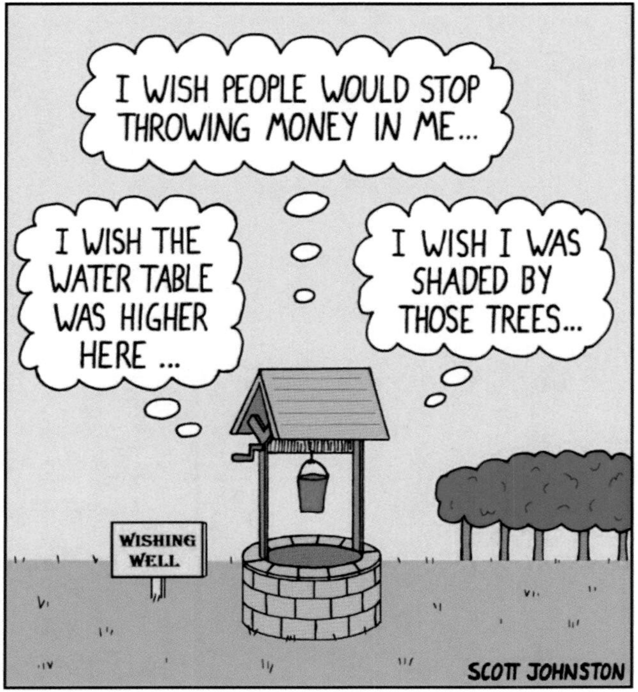
I WISH PEOPLE WOULD STOP THROWING MONEY IN ME...
I WISH THE WATER TABLE WAS HIGHER HERE ...
I WISH I WAS SHADED BY THOSE TREES...
WISHING WELL
SCOTT JOHNSTON

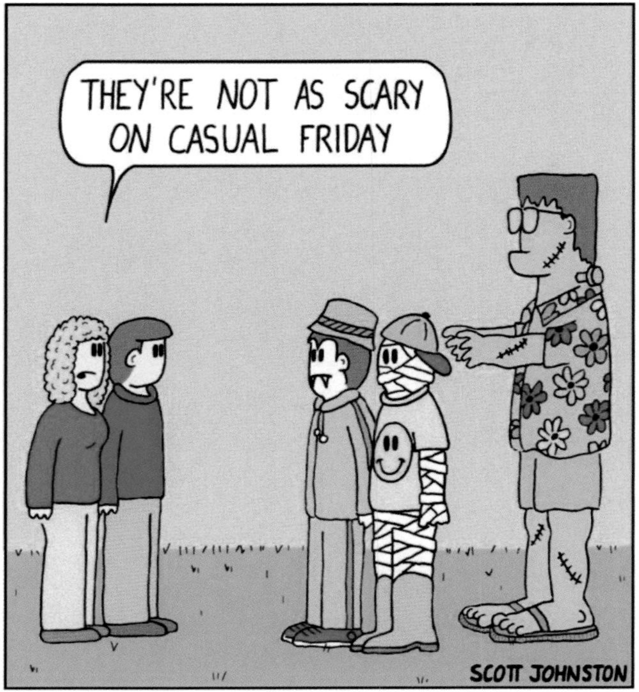
THEY'RE NOT AS SCARY ON CASUAL FRIDAY
SCOTT JOHNSTON

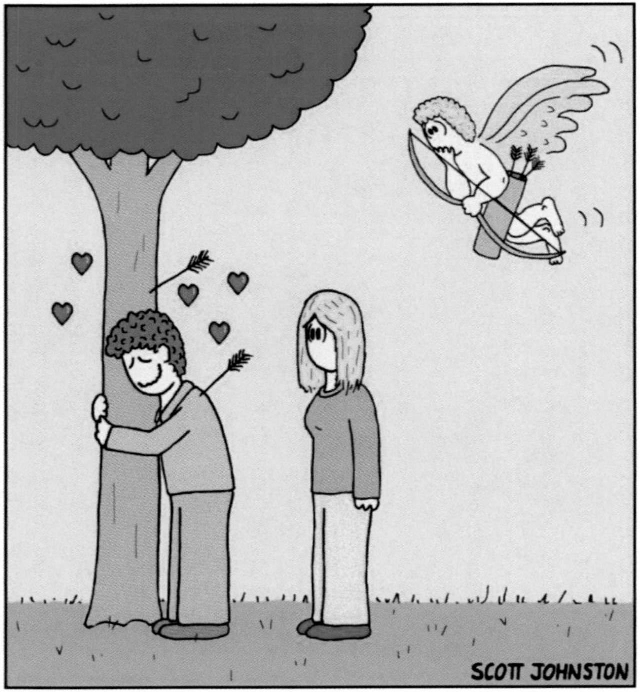
SCOTT JOHNSTON

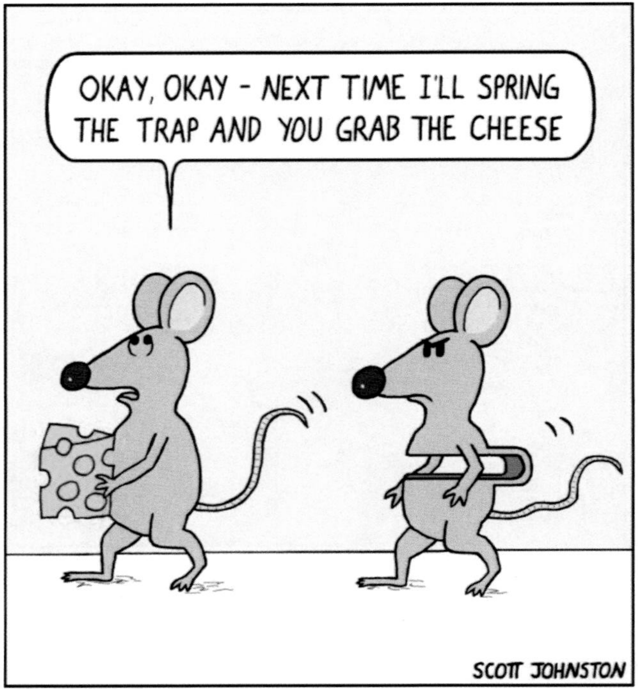
OKAY, OKAY - NEXT TIME I'LL SPRING THE TRAP AND YOU GRAB THE CHEESE
SCOTT JOHNSTON

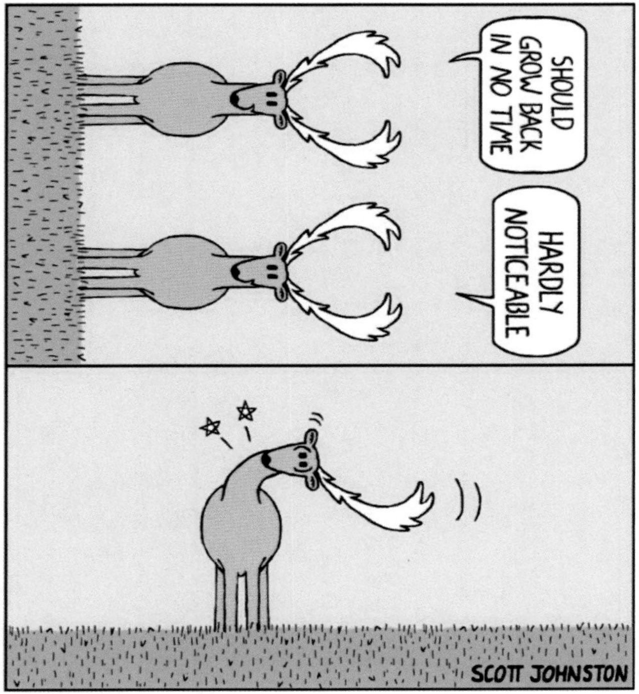
SHOULD GROW BACK IN NO TIME
HARDLY NOTICEABLE
SCOTT JOHNSTON

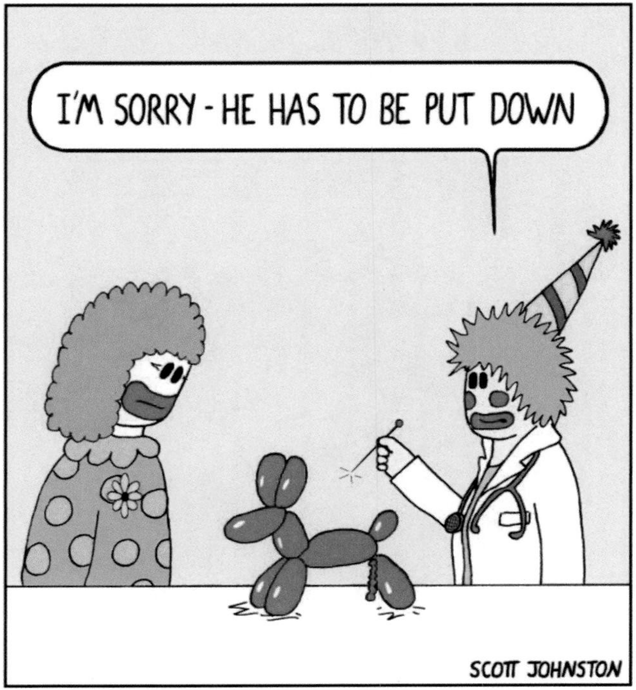
I'M SORRY - HE HAS TO BE PUT DOWN
SCOTT JOHNSTON

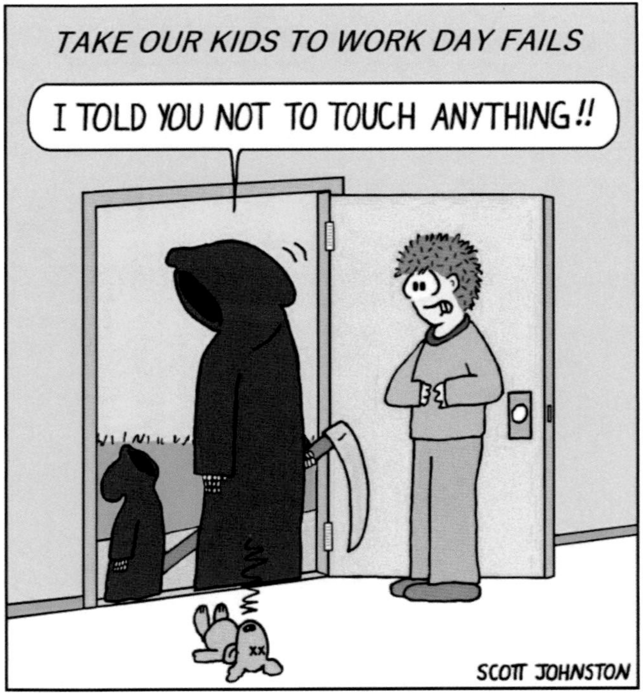
TAKE OUR KIDS TO WORK DAY FAILS
I TOLD YOU NOT TO TOUCH ANYTHING!!
SCOTT JOHNSTON

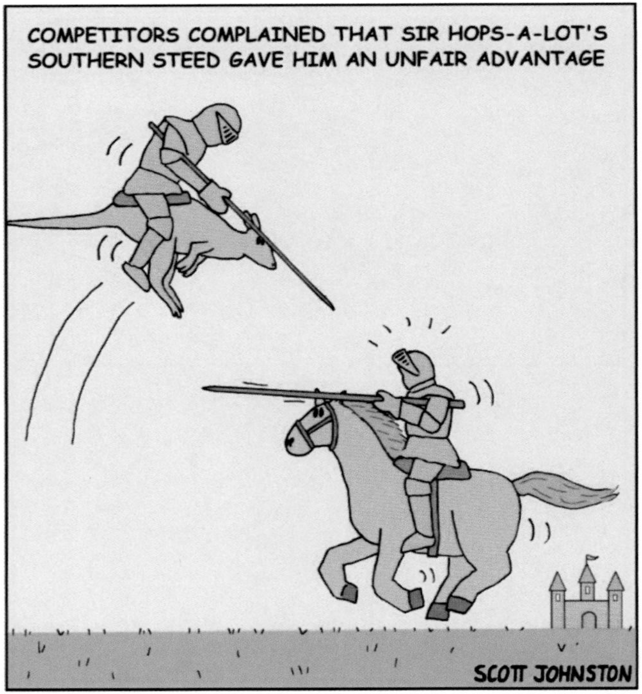
COMPETITORS COMPLAINED THAT SIR HOPS-A-LOT'S SOUTHERN STEED GAVE HIM AN UNFAIR ADVANTAGE
SCOTT JOHNSTON

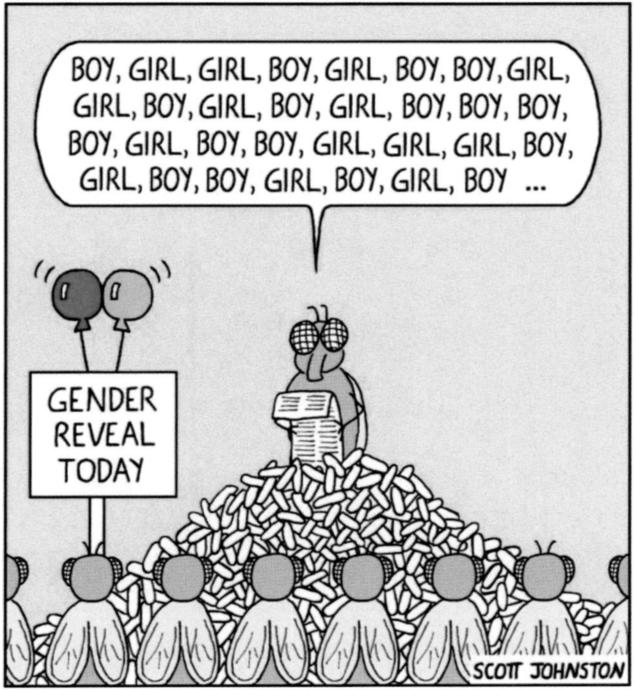
BOY, GIRL, GIRL, BOY, GIRL, BOY, BOY, GIRL, GIRL, BOY, GIRL, BOY, GIRL, BOY, BOY, BOY, BOY, GIRL, BOY, BOY, GIRL, GIRL, GIRL, BOY, GIRL, BOY, BOY, GIRL, BOY, GIRL, BOY ...
GENDER REVEAL TODAY
SCOTT JOHNSTON

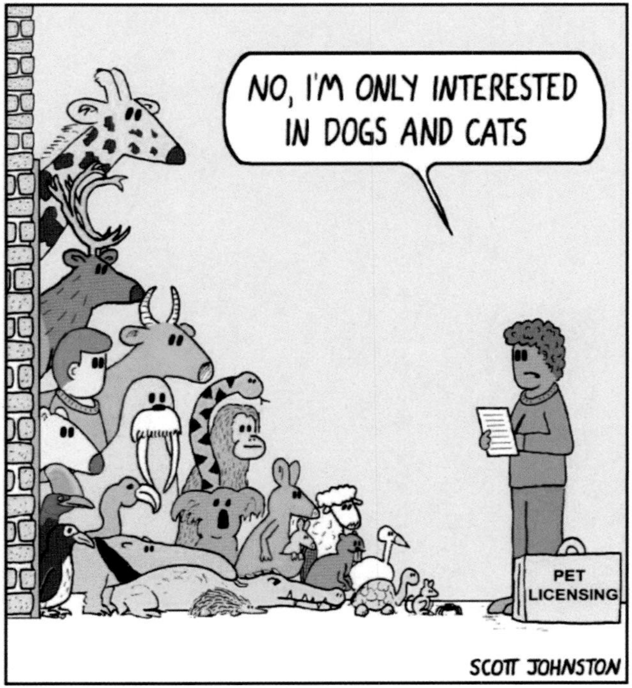
NO, I'M ONLY INTERESTED IN DOGS AND CATS
PET LICENSING
SCOTT JOHNSTON

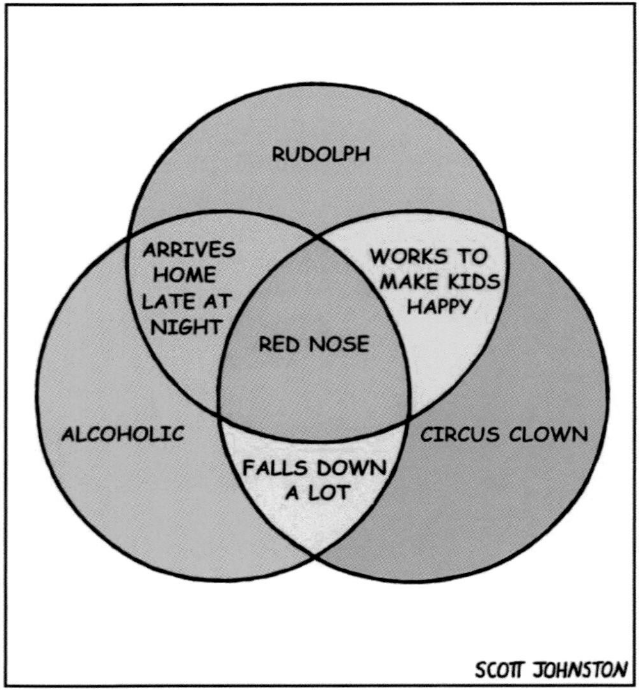
RUDOLPH
ARRIVES HOME LATE AT NIGHT
WORKS TO MAKE KIDS HAPPY
RED NOSE
ALCOHOLIC
CIRCUS CLOWN
FALLS DOWN A LOT
SCOTT JOHNSTON

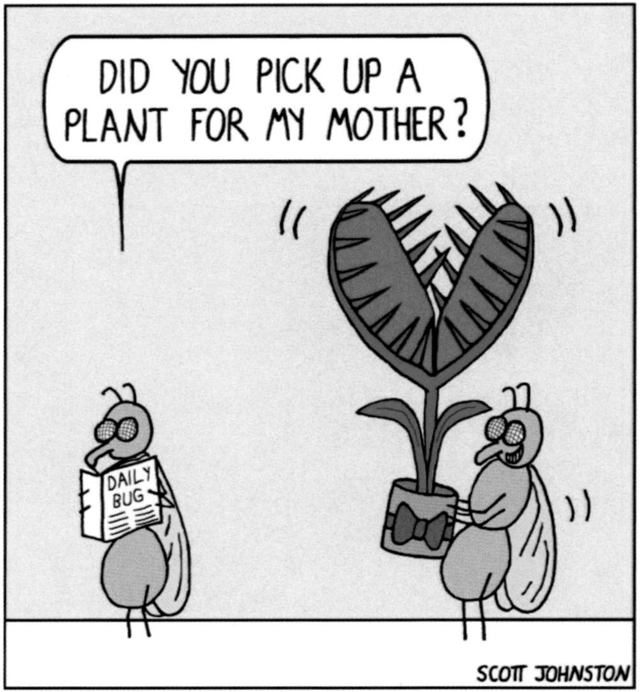
DID YOU PICK UP A PLANT FOR MY MOTHER?
DAILY BUG
SCOTT JOHNSTON

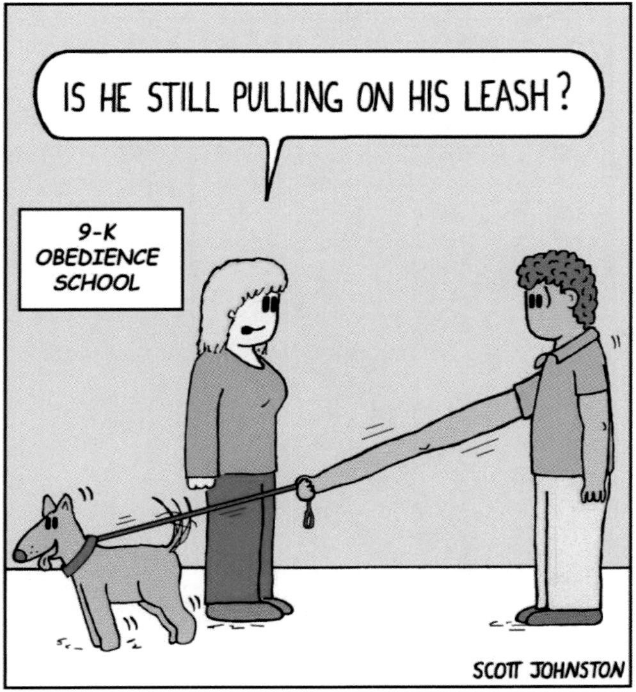
IS HE STILL PULLING ON HIS LEASH?
9-K OBEDIENCE SCHOOL
SCOTT JOHNSTON

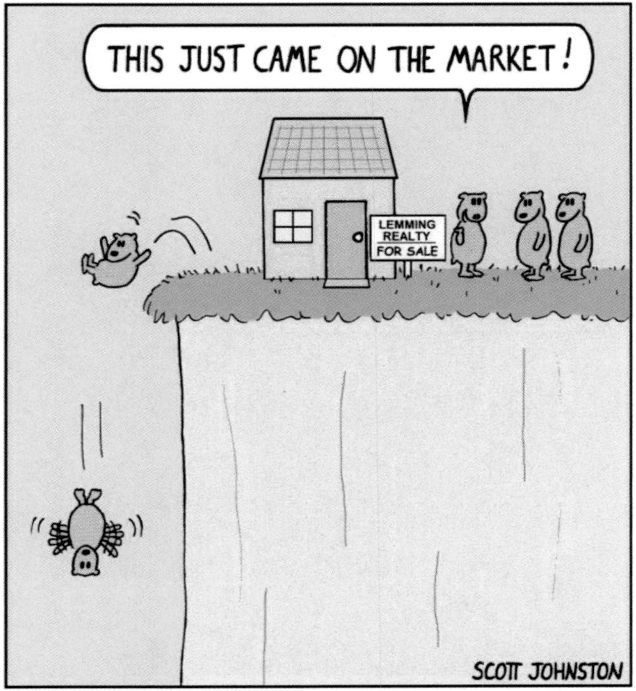
THIS JUST CAME ON THE MARKET!
LEMMING REALTY
FOR SALE
SCOTT JOHNSTON

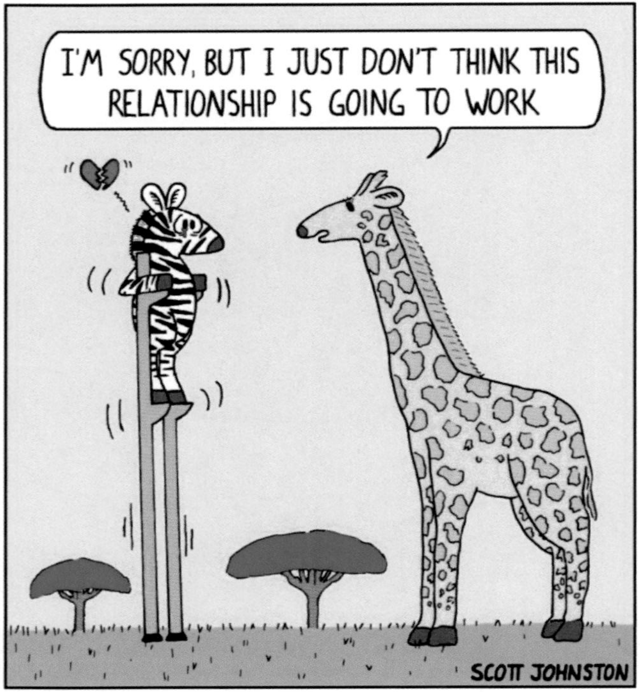
I'M SORRY, BUT I JUST DON'T THINK THIS RELATIONSHIP IS GOING TO WORK
SCOTT JOHNSTON

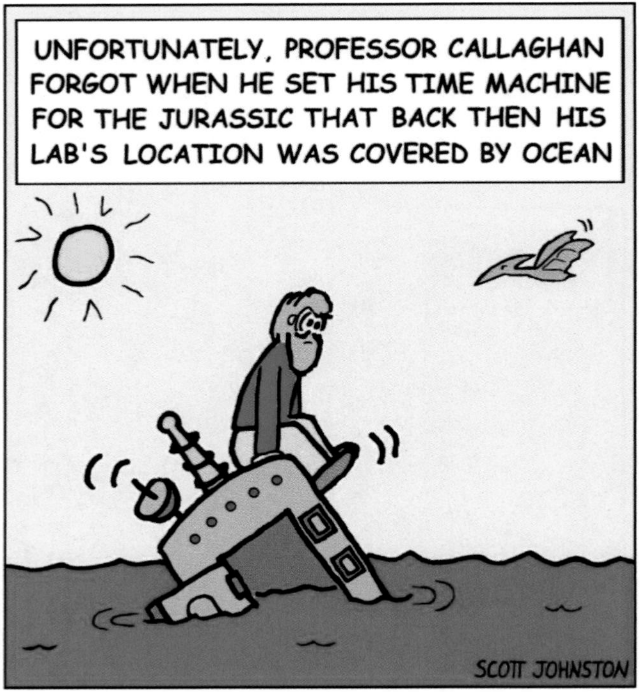
UNFORTUNATELY, PROFESSOR CALLAGHAN FORGOT WHEN HE SET HIS TIME MACHINE FOR THE JURASSIC THAT BACK THEN HIS LAB'S LOCATION WAS COVERED BY OCEAN
SCOTT JOHNSTON

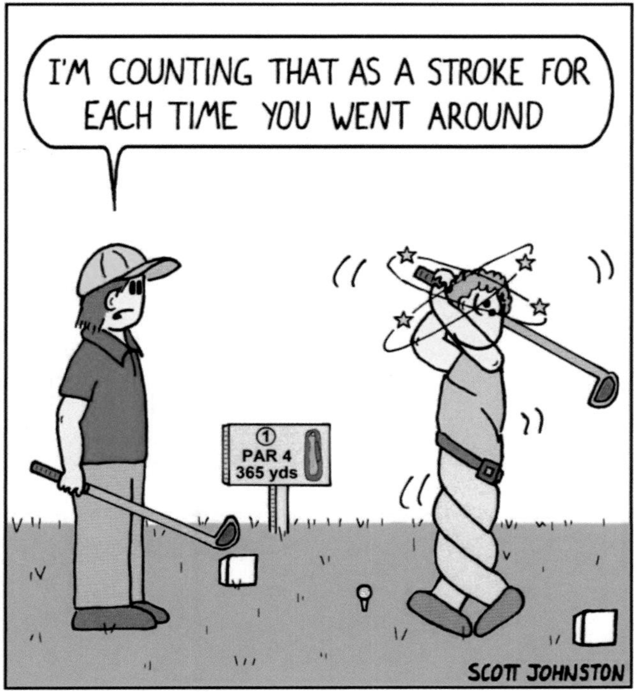
I'M COUNTING THAT AS A STROKE FOR EACH TIME YOU WENT AROUND
1
PAR 4
365 yds
SCOTT JOHNSTON

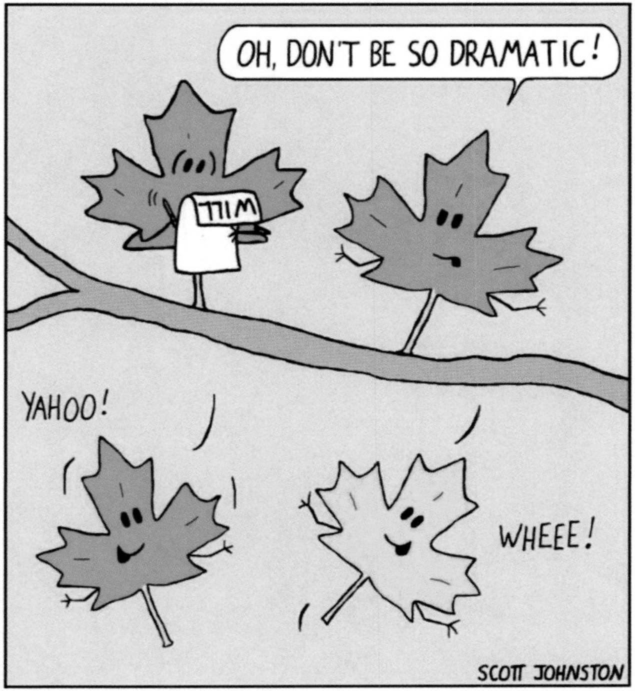
OH, DON'T BE SO DRAMATIC!
YAHOO!
WHEEE!
SCOTT JOHNSTON

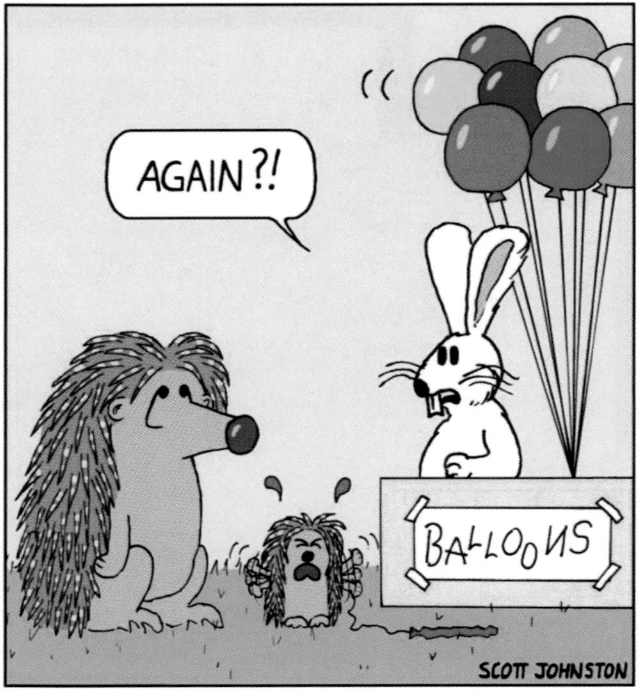
AGAIN?!
BALLOONS
SCOTT JOHNSTON

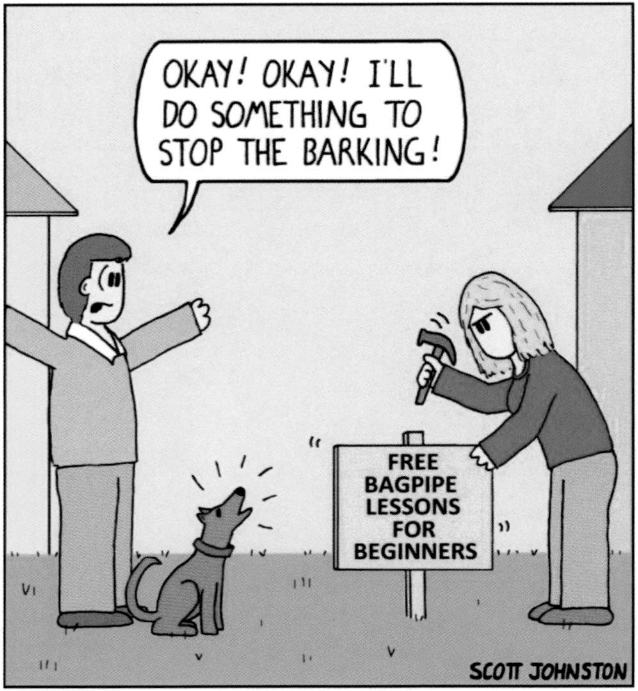
OKAY! OKAY! I'LL DO SOMETHING TO STOP THE BARKING!
FREE BAGPIPE LESSONS FOR BEGINNERS
SCOTT JOHNSTON

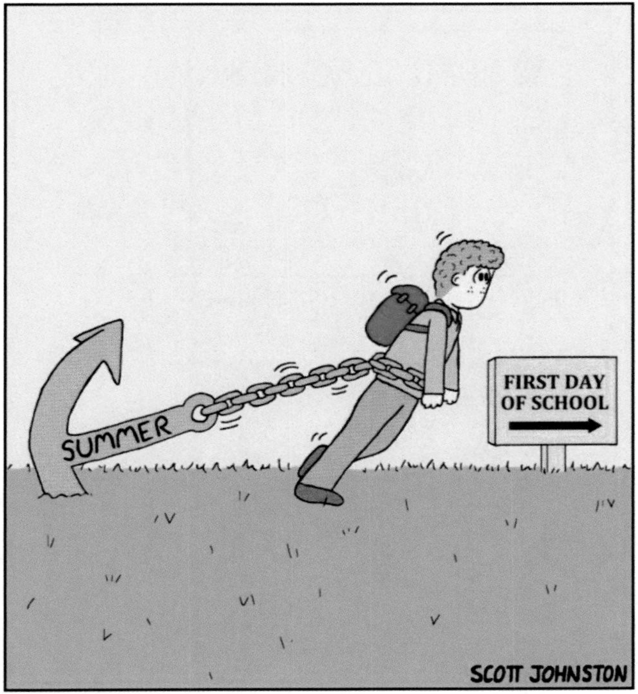
SUMMER
FIRST DAY OF SCHOOL
SCOTT JOHNSTON

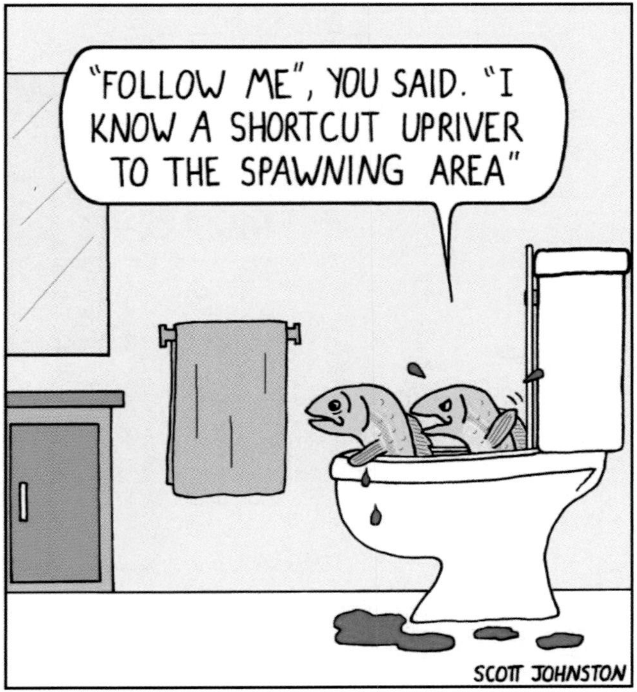
"FOLLOW ME", YOU SAID. "I KNOW A SHORTCUT UPRIVER TO THE SPAWNING AREA"
SCOTT JOHNSTON

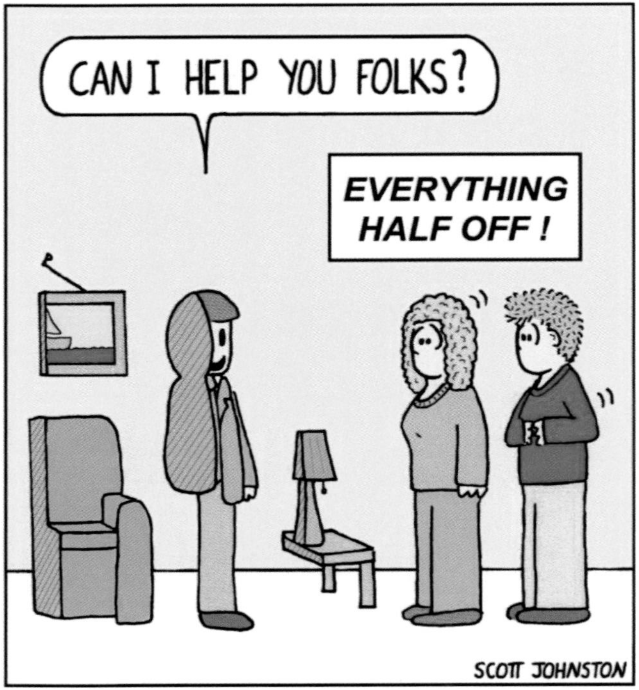
CAN I HELP YOU FOLKS?
EVERYTHING HALF OFF !
SCOTT JOHNSTON

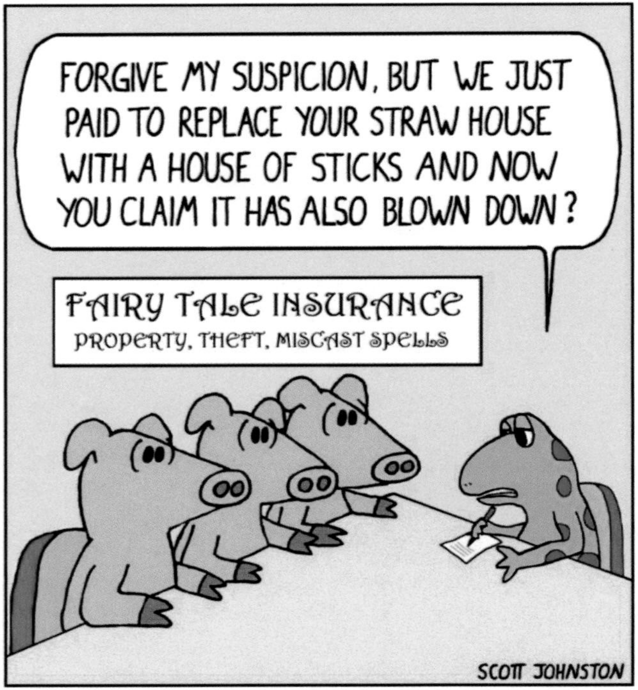
FORGIVE MY SUSPICION, BUT WE JUST PAID TO REPLACE YOUR STRAW HOUSE WITH A HOUSE OF STICKS AND NOW YOU CLAIM IT HAS ALSO BLOWN DOWN?
FAIRY TALE INSURANCE
PROPERTY, THEFT, MISCAST SPELLS
SCOTT JOHNSTON

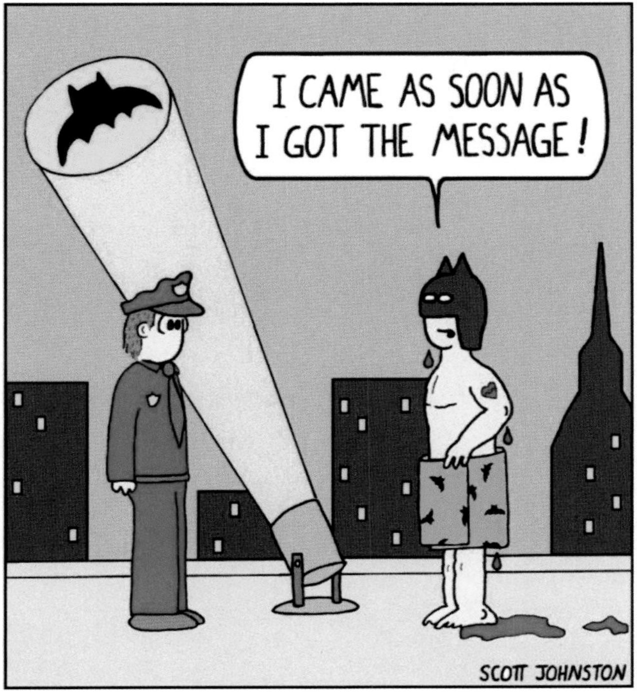
I CAME AS SOON AS I GOT THE MESSAGE!
SCOTT JOHNSTON

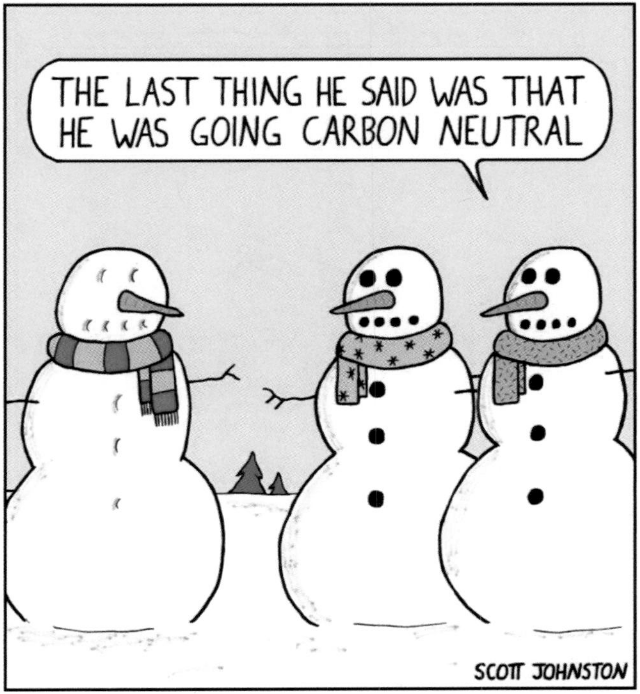
THE LAST THING HE SAID WAS THAT HE WAS GOING CARBON NEUTRAL
SCOTT JOHNSTON

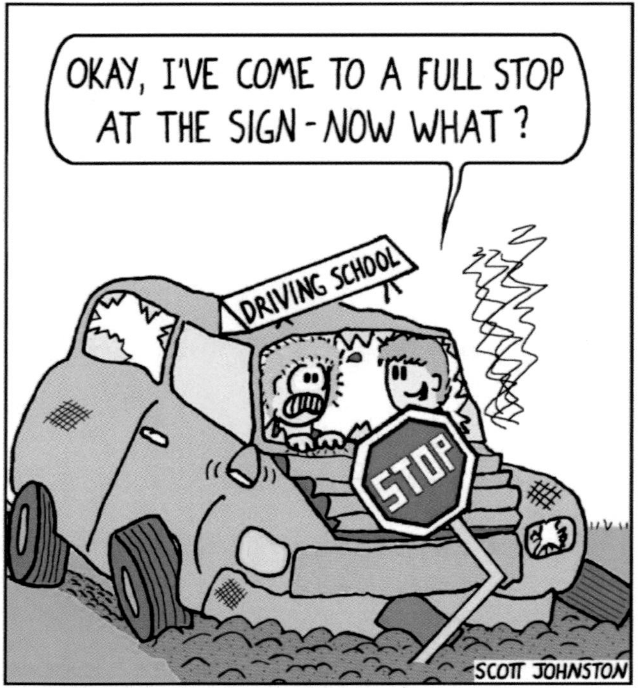
OKAY, I'VE COME TO A FULL STOP AT THE SIGN - NOW WHAT?
DRIVING SCHOOL
STOP
SCOTT JOHNSTON

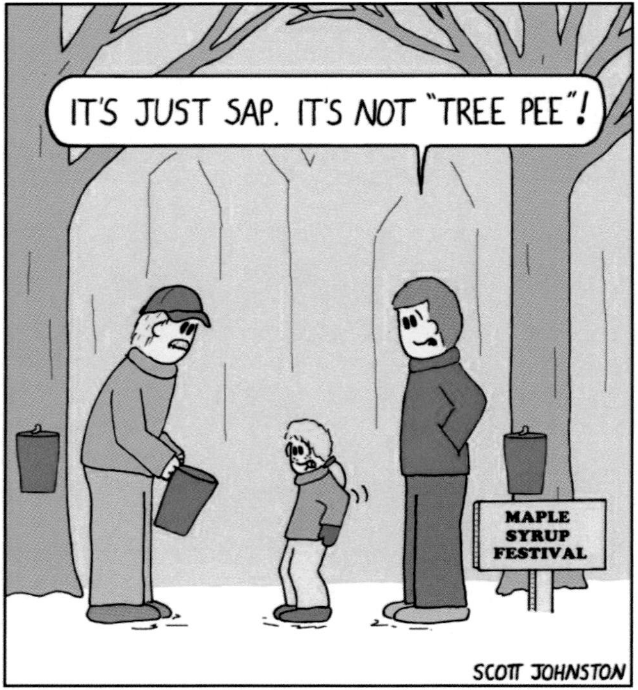
IT'S JUST SAP. IT'S NOT "TREE PEE"!
MAPLE SYRUP FESTIVAL
SCOTT JOHNSTON

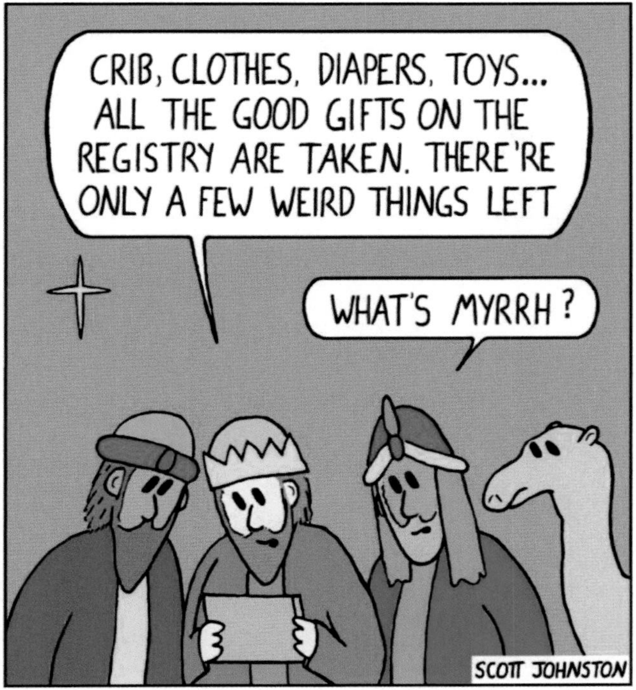
CRIB, CLOTHES, DIAPERS, TOYS... ALL THE GOOD GIFTS ON THE REGISTRY ARE TAKEN. THERE'RE ONLY A FEW WEIRD THINGS LEFT
WHAT'S MYRRH?
SCOTT JOHNSTON

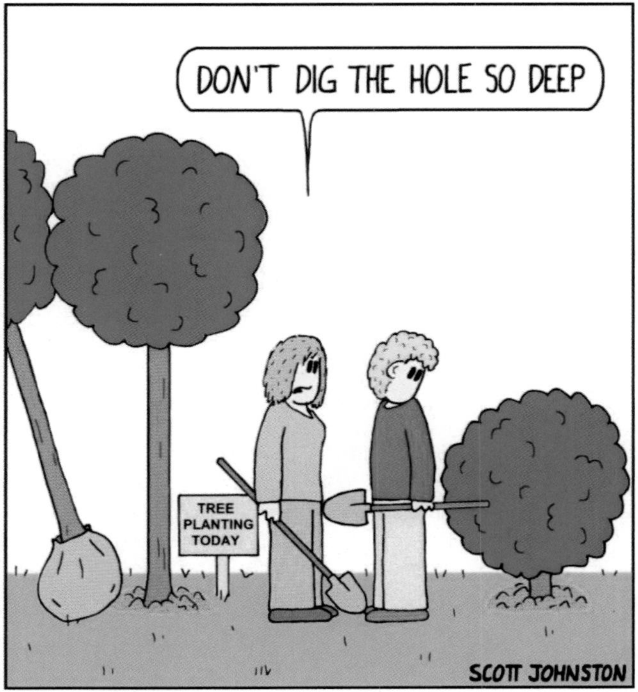
DON'T DIG THE HOLE SO DEEP
TREE PLANTING TODAY
SCOTT JOHNSTON

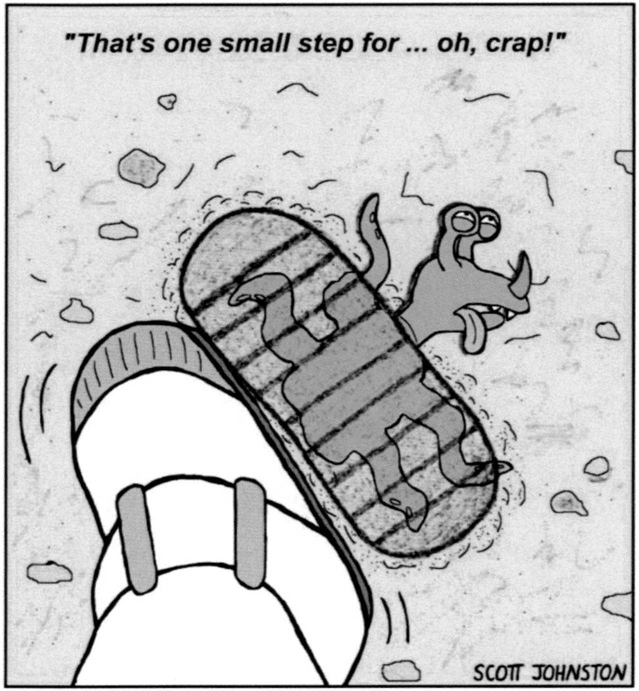
"That's one small step for ... oh, crap!"
SCOTT JOHNSTON

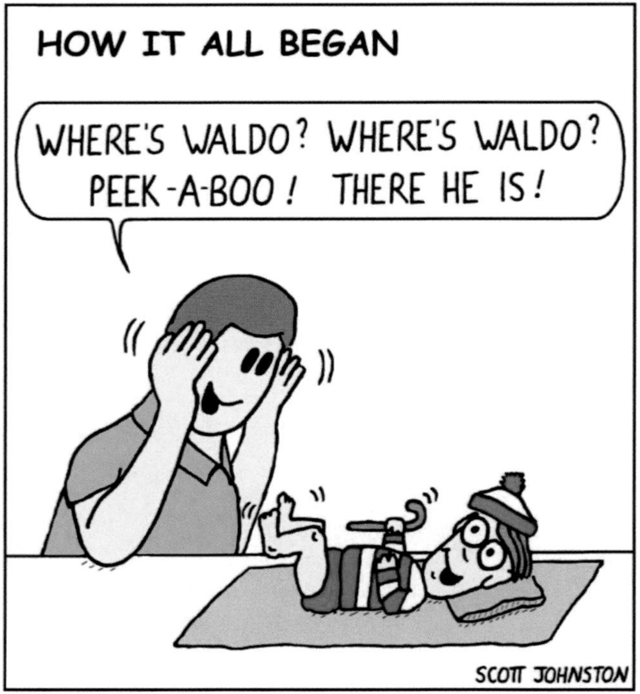
HOW IT ALL BEGAN
WHERE'S WALDO? WHERE'S WALDO? PEEK-A-BOO! THERE HE IS!
SCOTT JOHNSTON

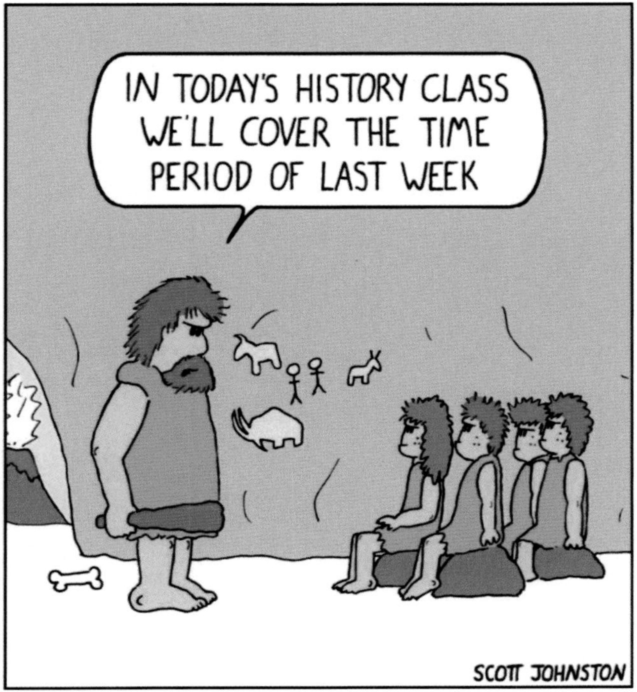
IN TODAY'S HISTORY CLASS WE'LL COVER THE TIME PERIOD OF LAST WEEK
SCOTT JOHNSTON

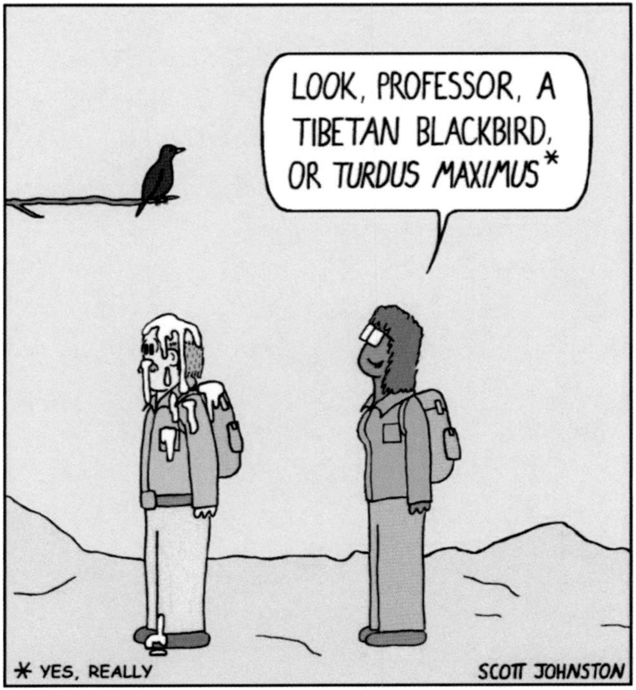
LOOK, PROFESSOR, A TIBETAN BLACKBIRD, OR *TURDUS MAXIMUS**
* YES, REALLY
SCOTT JOHNSTON

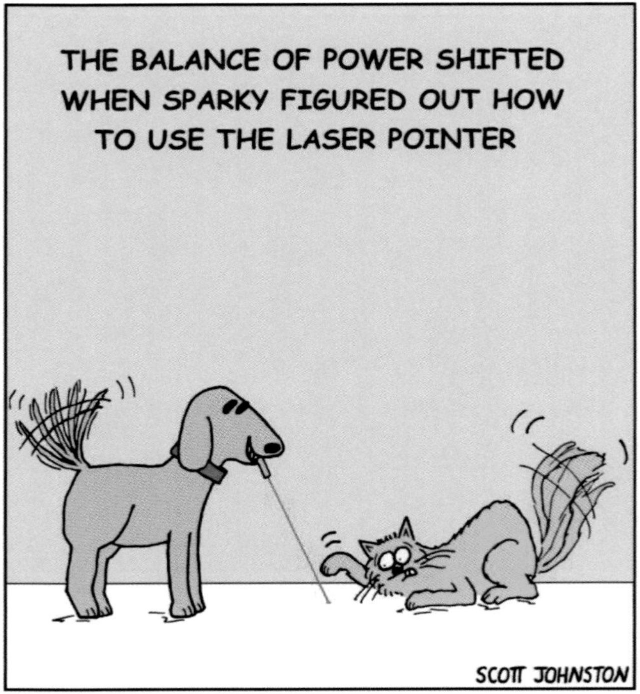
THE BALANCE OF POWER SHIFTED WHEN SPARKY FIGURED OUT HOW TO USE THE LASER POINTER
SCOTT JOHNSTON

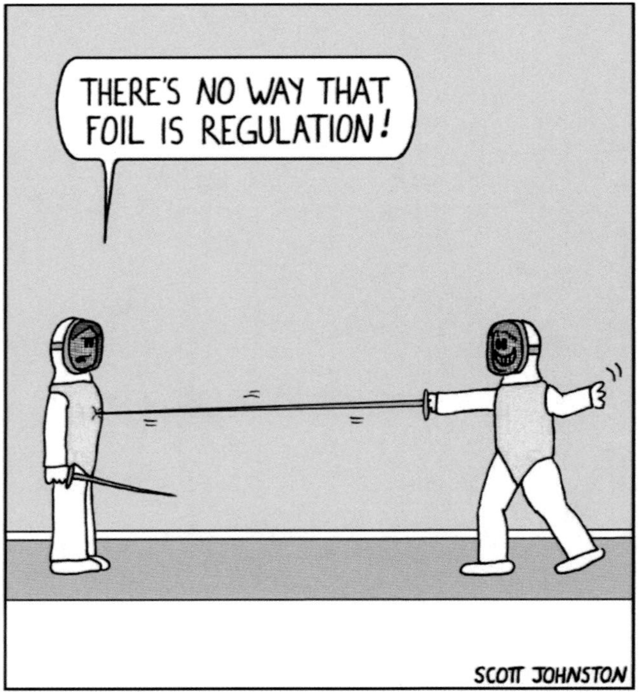
THERE'S NO WAY THAT FOIL IS REGULATION!
SCOTT JOHNSTON

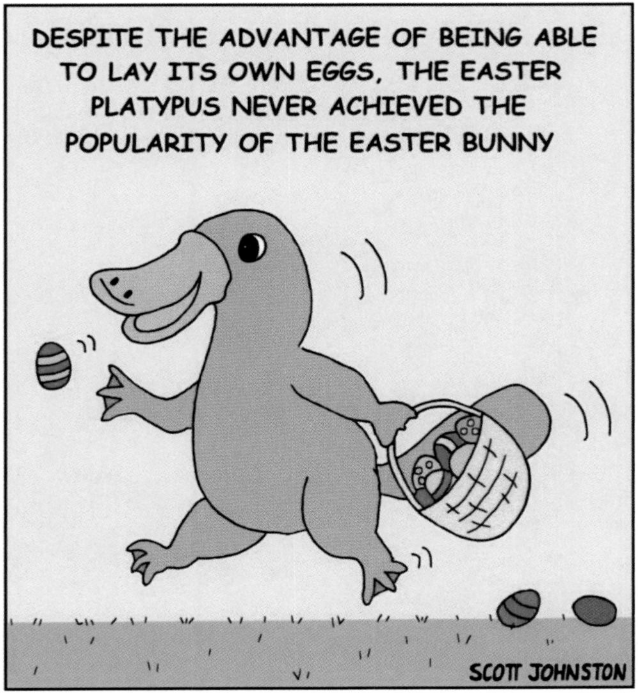
DESPITE THE ADVANTAGE OF BEING ABLE TO LAY ITS OWN EGGS, THE EASTER PLATYPUS NEVER ACHIEVED THE POPULARITY OF THE EASTER BUNNY
SCOTT JOHNSTON

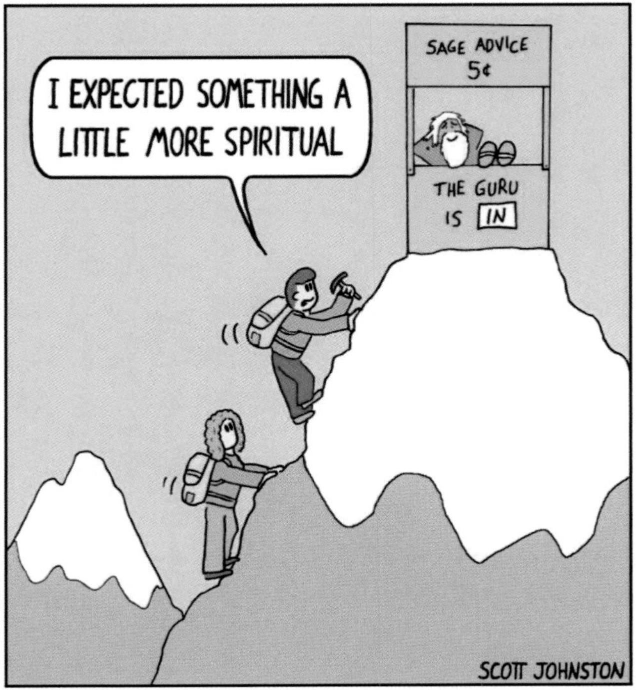
I EXPECTED SOMETHING A LITTLE MORE SPIRITUAL
SAGE ADVICE 5¢
THE GURU IS IN
SCOTT JOHNSTON

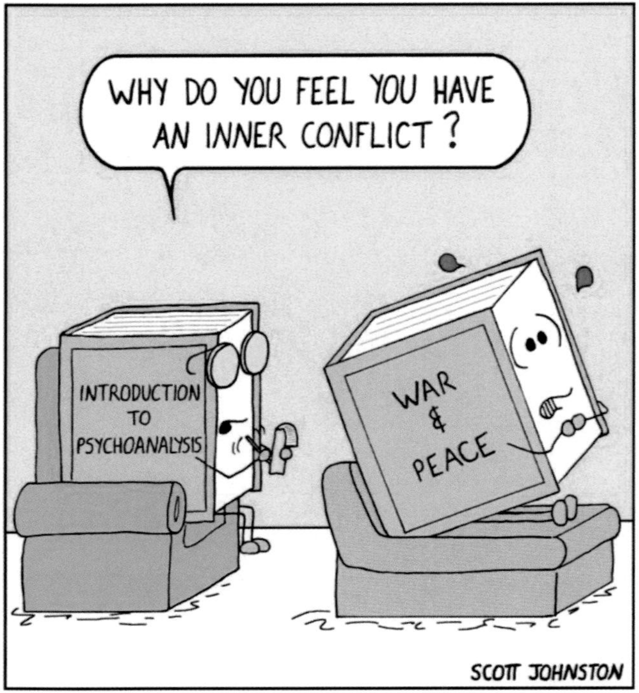
WHY DO YOU FEEL YOU HAVE AN INNER CONFLICT?
INTRODUCTION TO PSYCHOANALYSIS
WAR & PEACE
SCOTT JOHNSTON

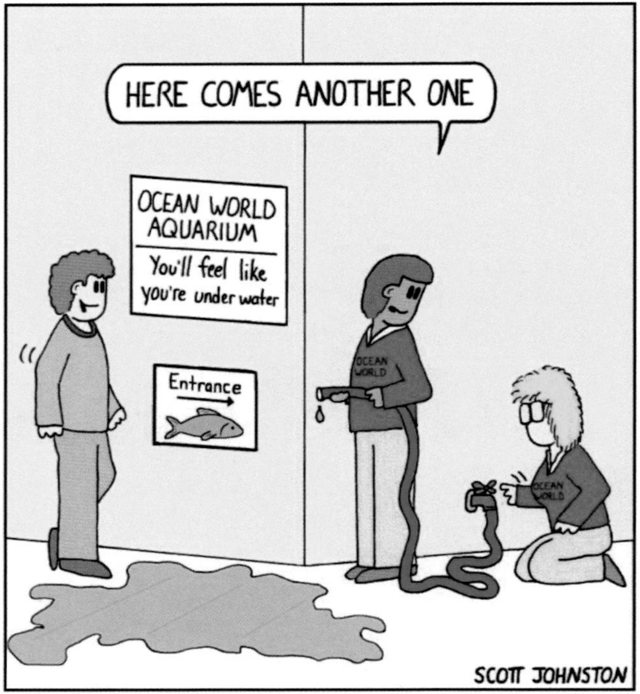
HERE COMES ANOTHER ONE
OCEAN WORLD AQUARIUM
You'll feel like you're under water
Entrance
OCEAN WORLD
OCEAN WORLD
SCOTT JOHNSTON

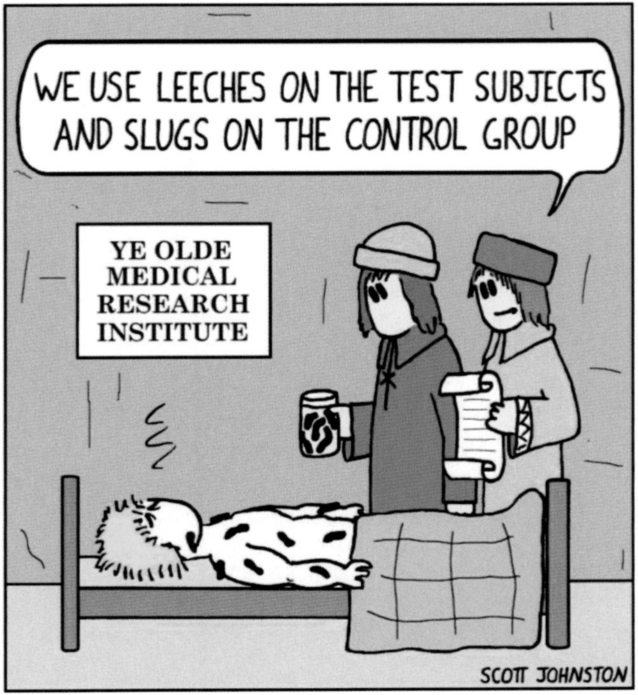
WE USE LEECHES ON THE TEST SUBJECTS AND SLUGS ON THE CONTROL GROUP
YE OLDE MEDICAL RESEARCH INSTITUTE
SCOTT JOHNSTON

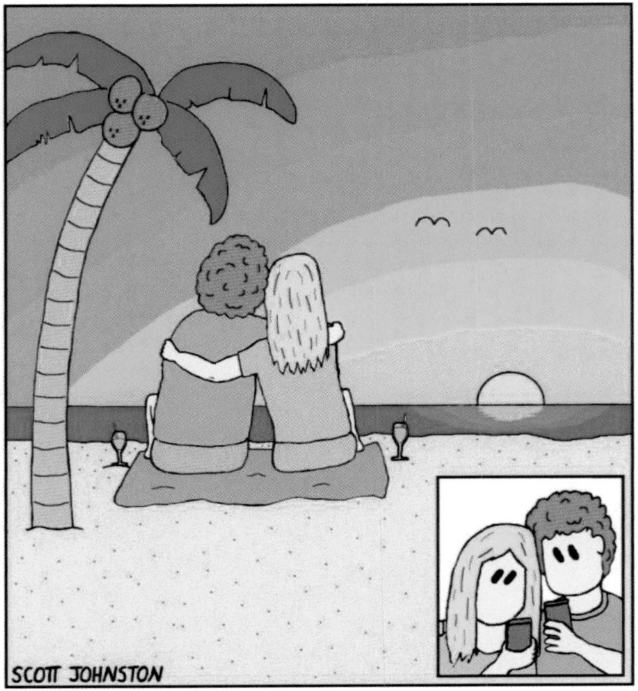
SCOTT JOHNSTON

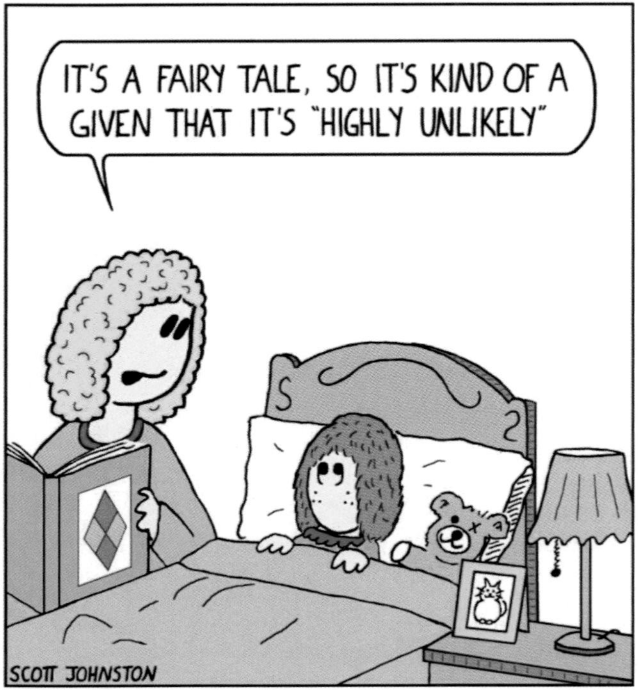
IT'S A FAIRY TALE, SO IT'S KIND OF A GIVEN THAT IT'S "HIGHLY UNLIKELY"
SCOTT JOHNSTON

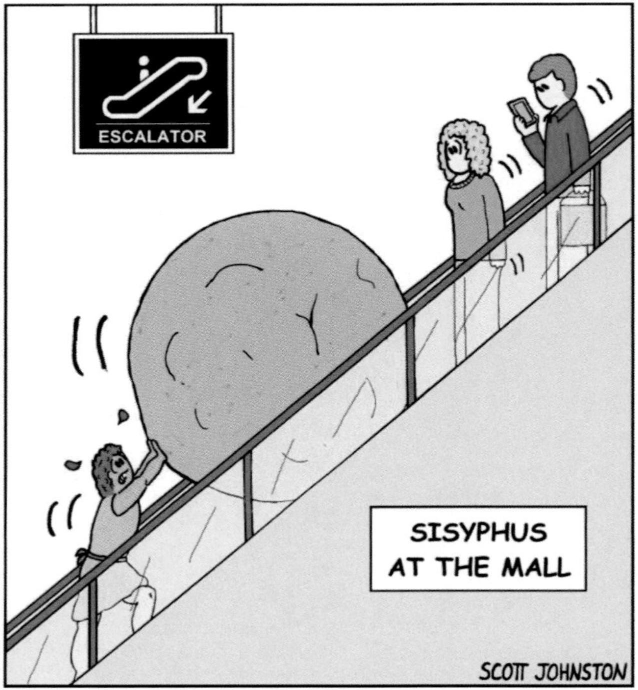
ESCALATOR
SISYPHUS AT THE MALL
SCOTT JOHNSTON

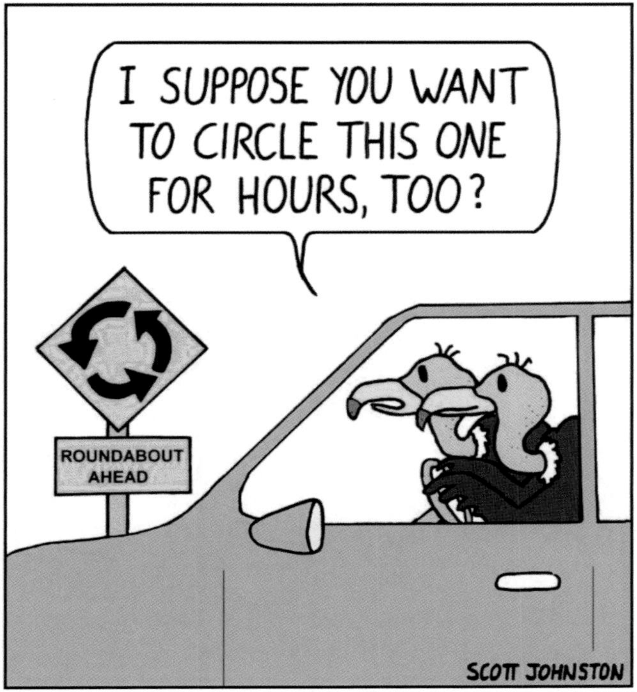
I SUPPOSE YOU WANT TO CIRCLE THIS ONE FOR HOURS, TOO?
ROUNDABOUT AHEAD
SCOTT JOHNSTON

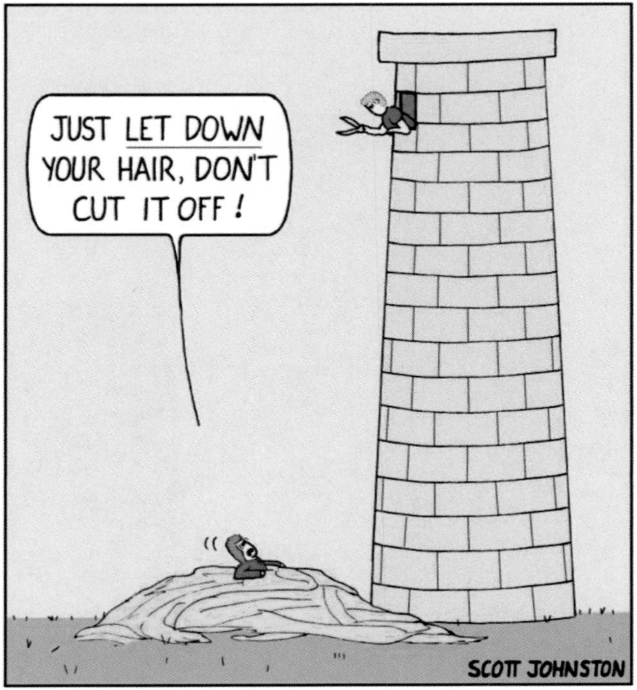
JUST LET DOWN YOUR HAIR, DON'T CUT IT OFF!
SCOTT JOHNSTON

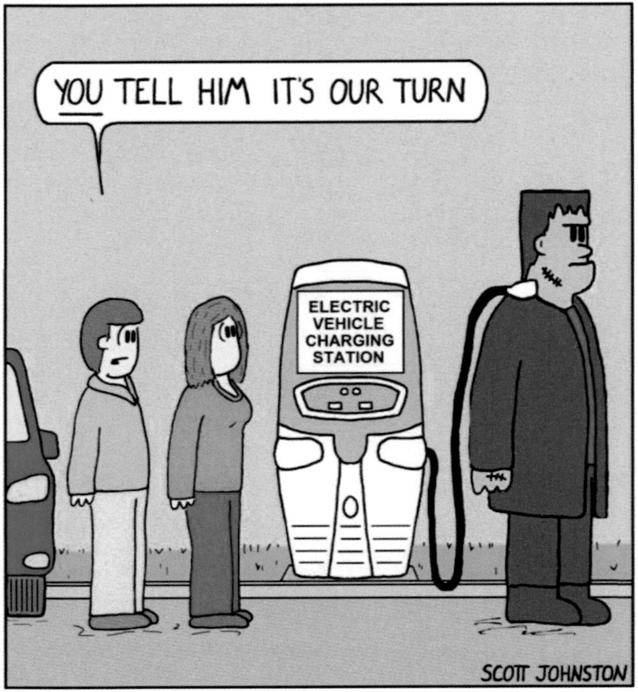
YOU TELL HIM IT'S OUR TURN
ELECTRIC VEHICLE CHARGING STATION
SCOTT JOHNSTON

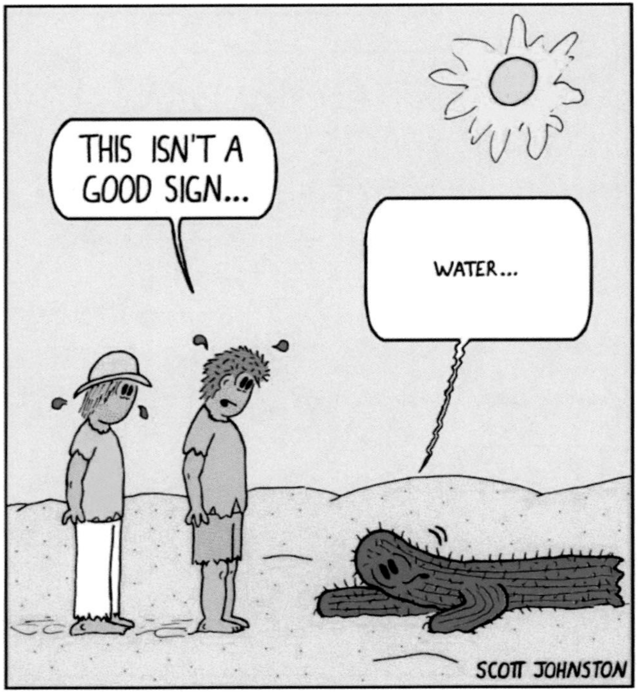
THIS ISN'T A GOOD SIGN...
WATER...
SCOTT JOHNSTON

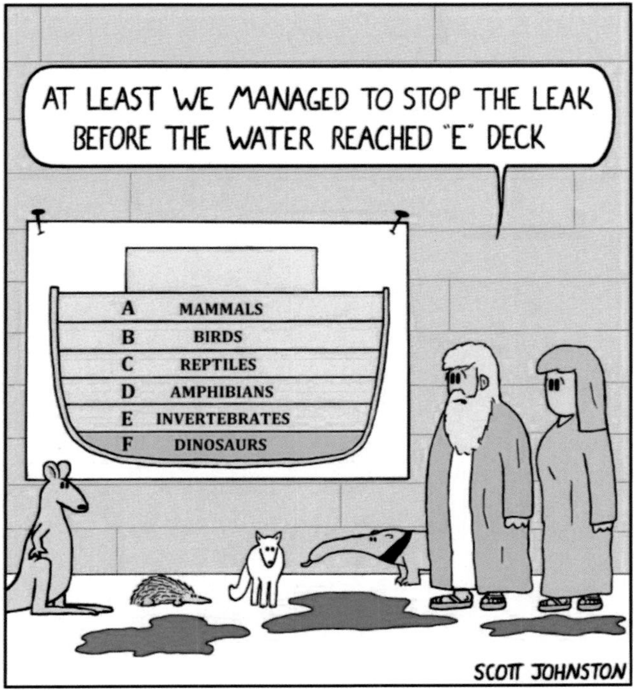
AT LEAST WE MANAGED TO STOP THE LEAK BEFORE THE WATER REACHED "E" DECK
A MAMMALS
B BIRDS
C REPTILES
D AMPHIBIANS
E INVERTEBRATES
F DINOSAURS
SCOTT JOHNSTON

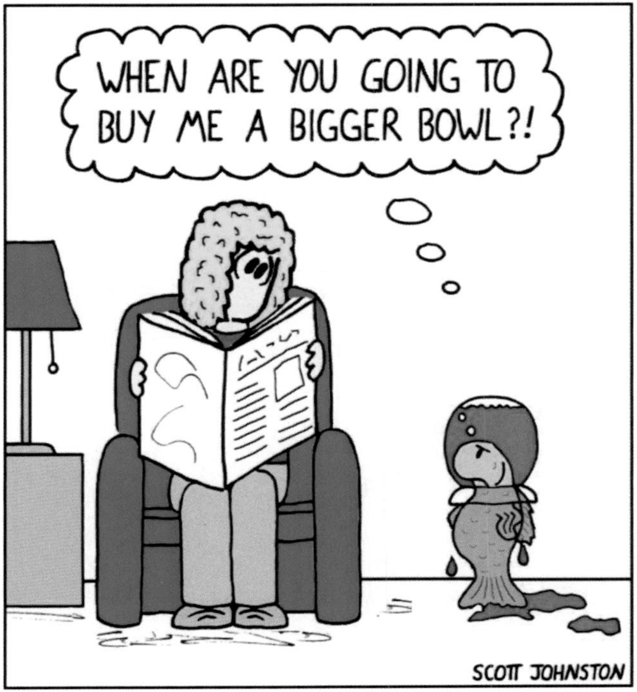
WHEN ARE YOU GOING TO BUY ME A BIGGER BOWL?!
SCOTT JOHNSTON

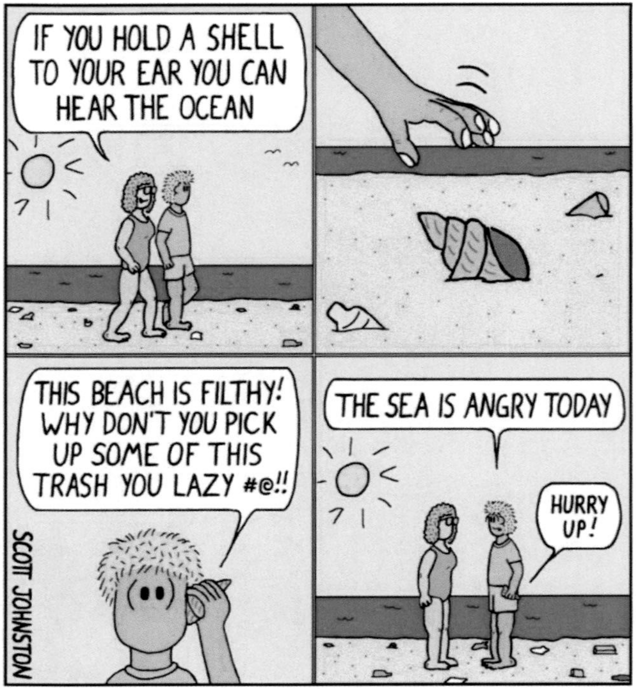
IF YOU HOLD A SHELL TO YOUR EAR YOU CAN HEAR THE OCEAN
THIS BEACH IS FILTHY! WHY DON'T YOU PICK UP SOME OF THIS TRASH YOU LAZY #@!!
THE SEA IS ANGRY TODAY
HURRY UP!
SCOTT JOHNSTON

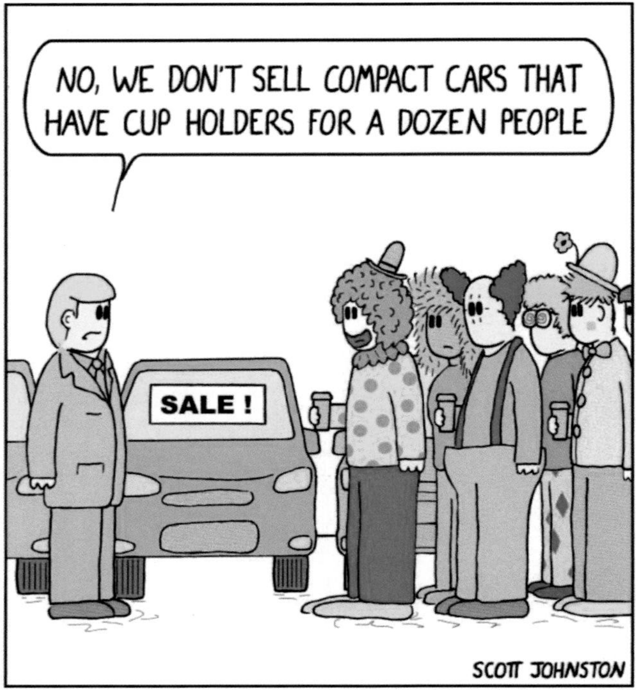
NO, WE DON'T SELL COMPACT CARS THAT HAVE CUP HOLDERS FOR A DOZEN PEOPLE
SALE !
SCOTT JOHNSTON

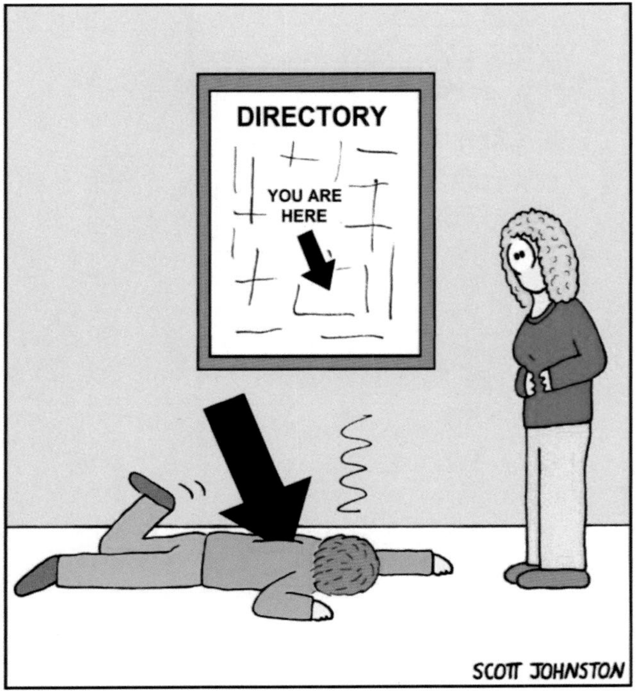
DIRECTORY
YOU ARE HERE
SCOTT JOHNSTON

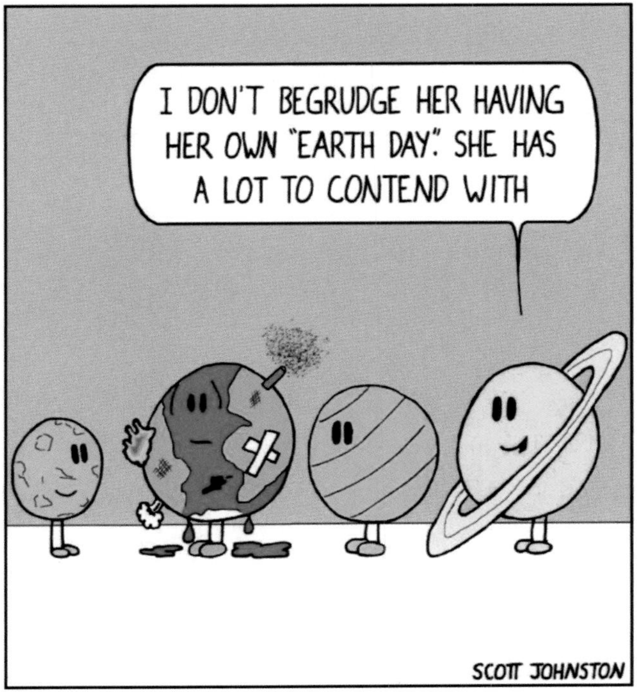
I DON'T BEGRUDGE HER HAVING HER OWN "EARTH DAY." SHE HAS A LOT TO CONTEND WITH
SCOTT JOHNSTON

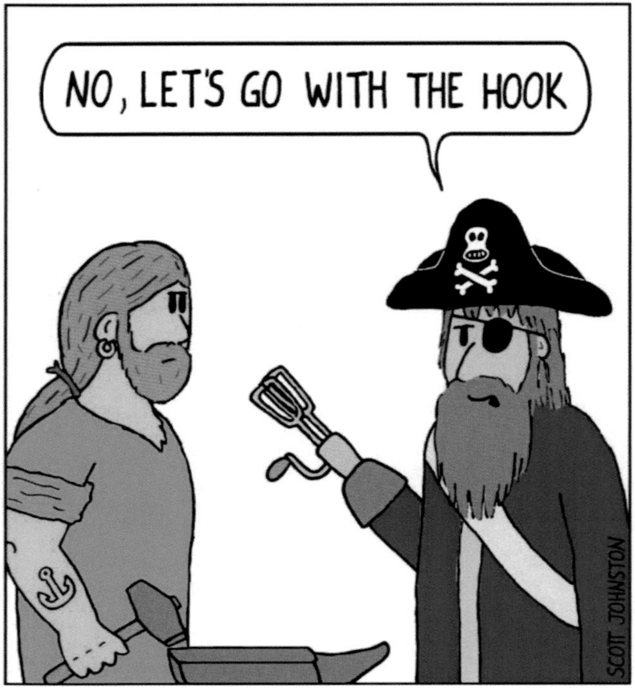
NO, LET'S GO WITH THE HOOK
SCOTT JOHNSTON

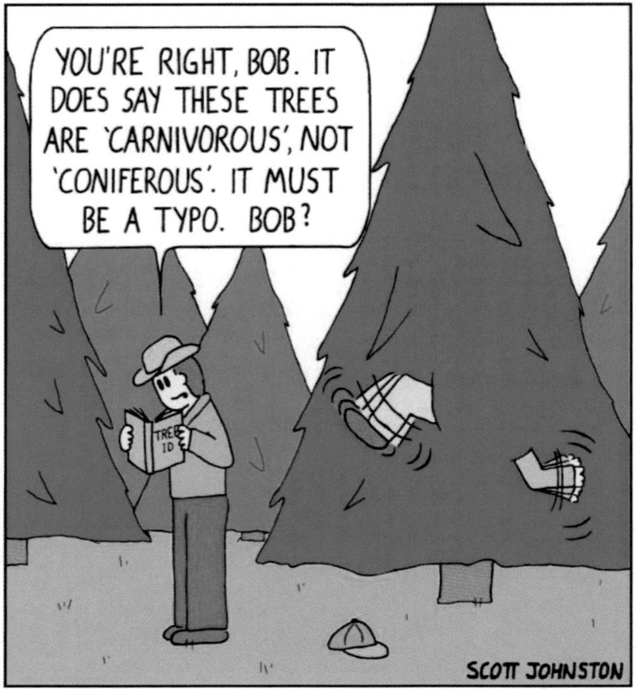
YOU'RE RIGHT, BOB. IT DOES SAY THESE TREES ARE 'CARNIVOROUS', NOT 'CONIFEROUS'. IT MUST BE A TYPO. BOB?
TREE ID
SCOTT JOHNSTON

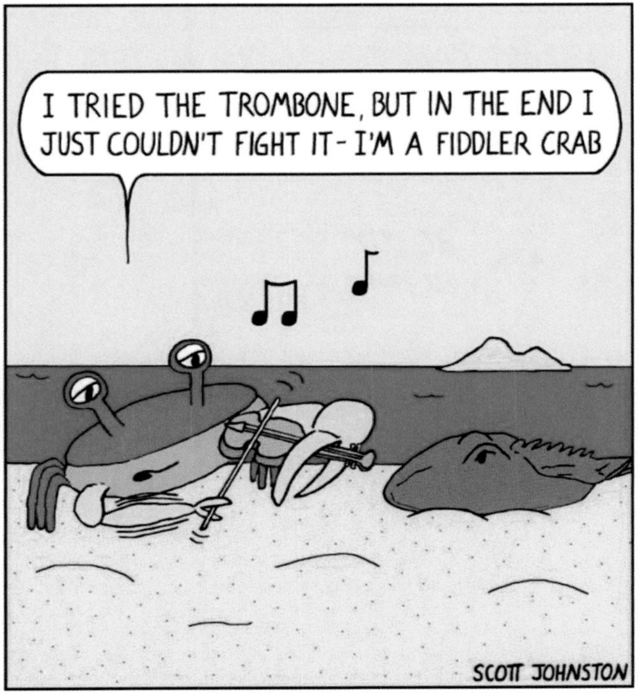
I TRIED THE TROMBONE, BUT IN THE END I JUST COULDN'T FIGHT IT - I'M A FIDDLER CRAB
SCOTT JOHNSTON

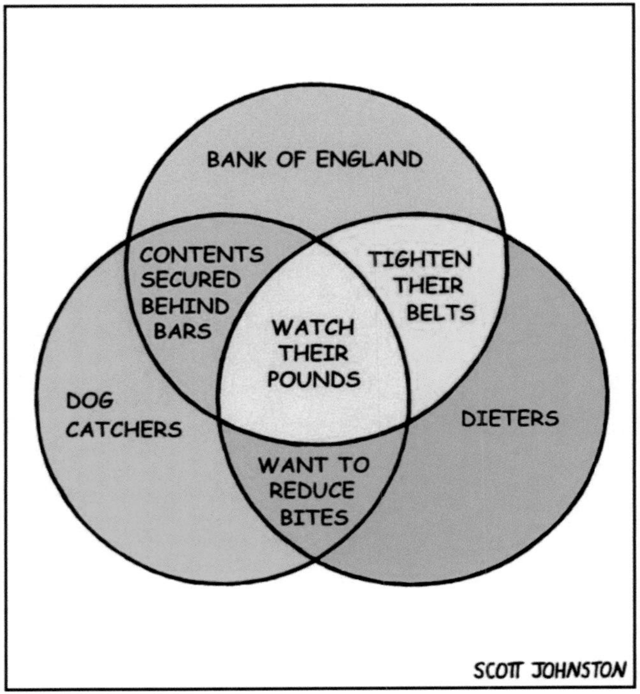
BANK OF ENGLAND
CONTENTS SECURED BEHIND BARS
TIGHTEN THEIR BELTS
WATCH THEIR POUNDS
DOG CATCHERS
DIETERS
WANT TO REDUCE BITES
SCOTT JOHNSTON

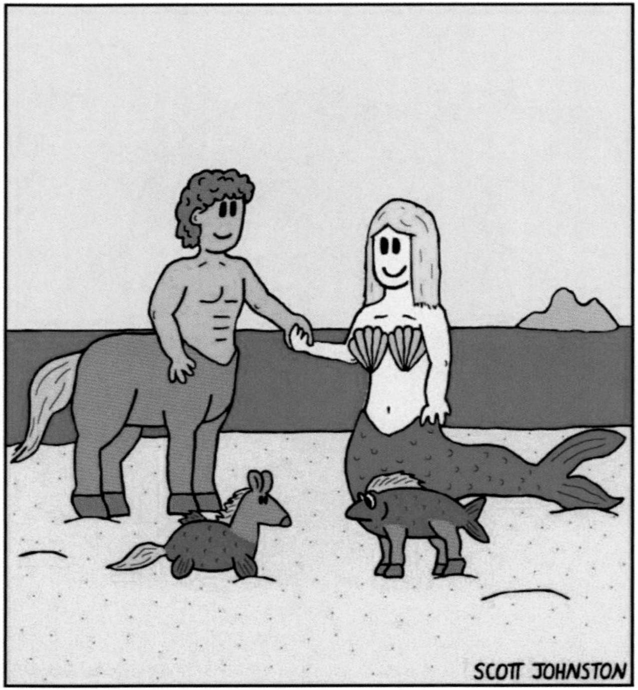
SCOTT JOHNSTON

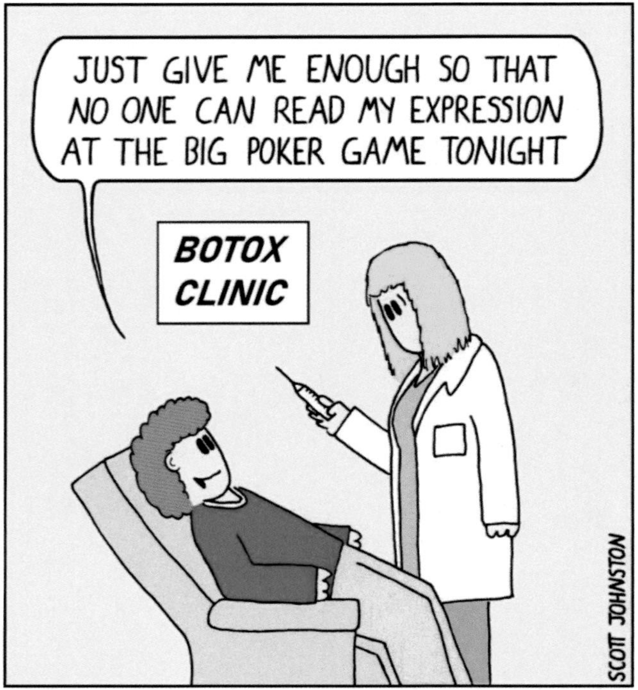
JUST GIVE ME ENOUGH SO THAT NO ONE CAN READ MY EXPRESSION AT THE BIG POKER GAME TONIGHT
BOTOX CLINIC
SCOTT JOHNSTON

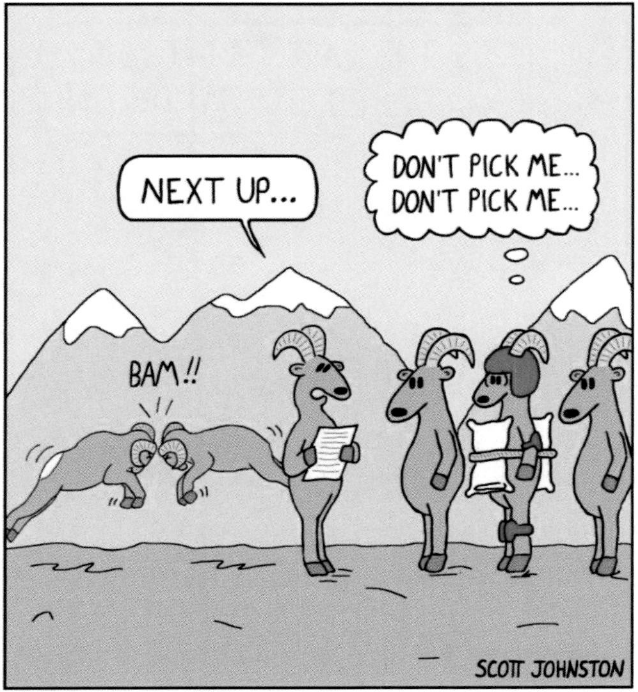
NEXT UP...
DON'T PICK ME...
DON'T PICK ME...
BAM!!
SCOTT JOHNSTON

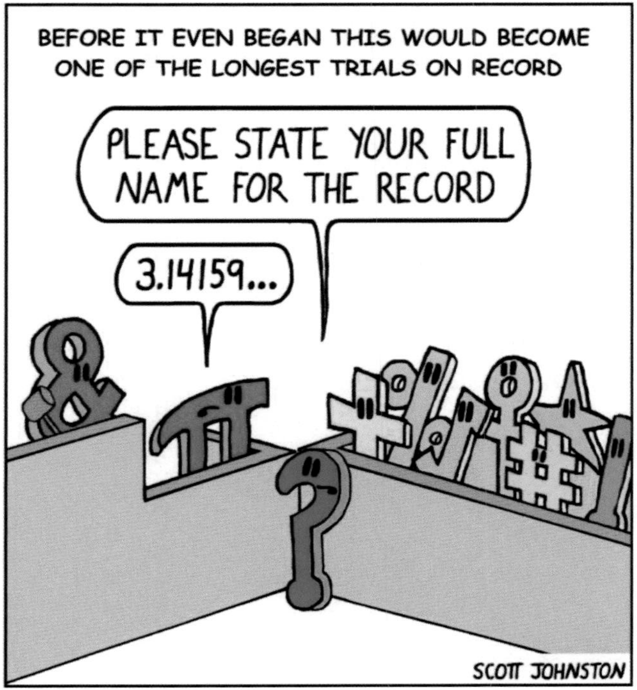
BEFORE IT EVEN BEGAN THIS WOULD BECOME ONE OF THE LONGEST TRIALS ON RECORD
PLEASE STATE YOUR FULL NAME FOR THE RECORD
3.14159...
SCOTT JOHNSTON

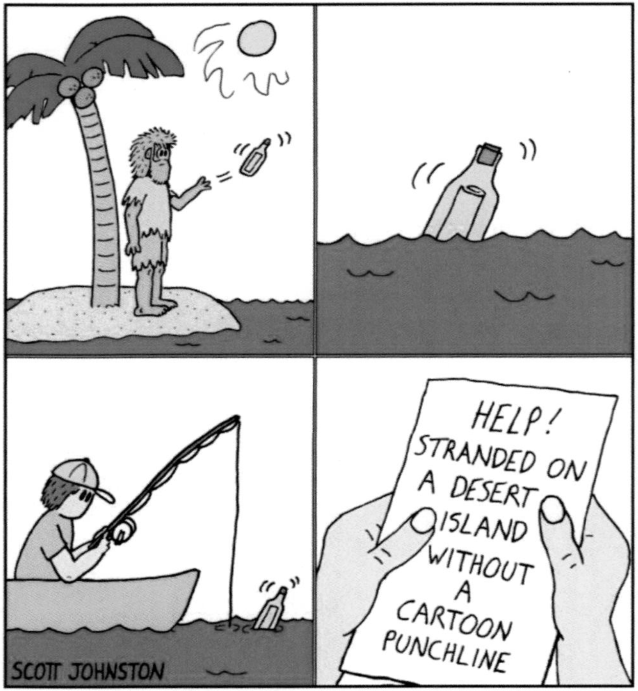
HELP!
STRANDED ON A DESERT ISLAND WITHOUT A CARTOON PUNCHLINE
SCOTT JOHNSTON

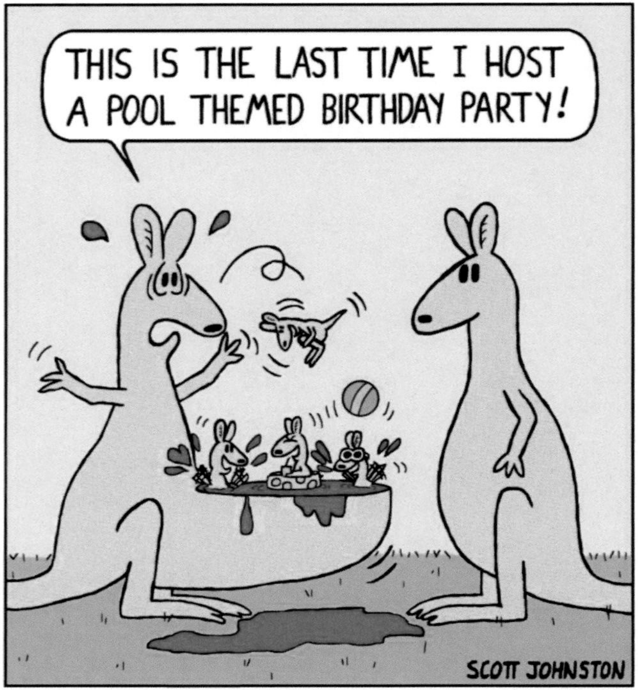
THIS IS THE LAST TIME I HOST A POOL THEMED BIRTHDAY PARTY!
SCOTT JOHNSTON

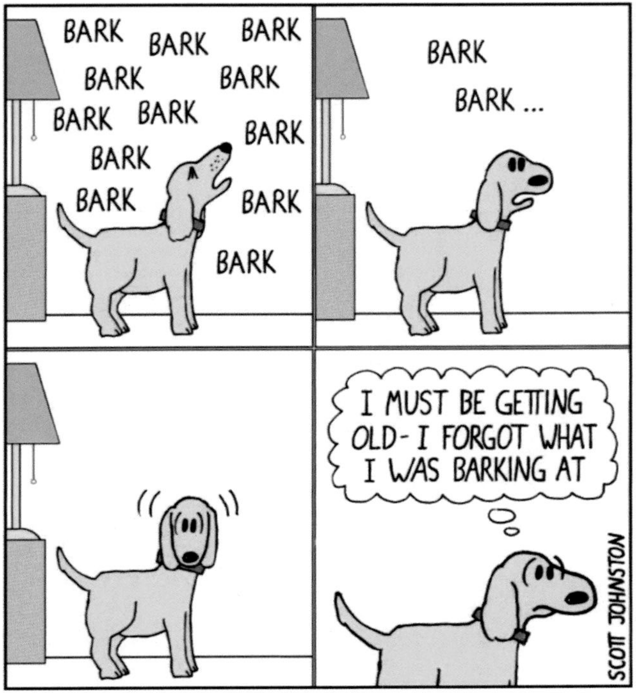
BARK BARK BARK BARK BARK BARK BARK BARK BARK BARK BARK BARK
BARK
BARK ...
I MUST BE GETTING OLD- I FORGOT WHAT I WAS BARKING AT
SCOTT JOHNSTON

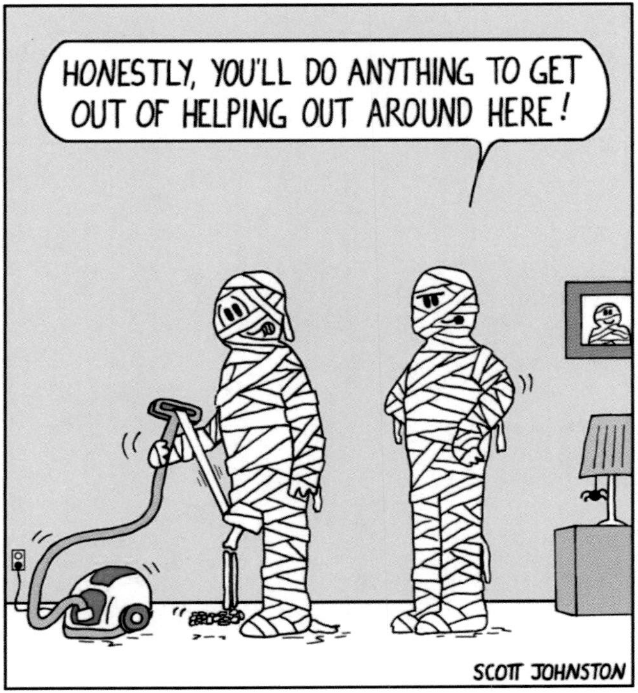
HONESTLY, YOU'LL DO ANYTHING TO GET OUT OF HELPING OUT AROUND HERE!
SCOTT JOHNSTON

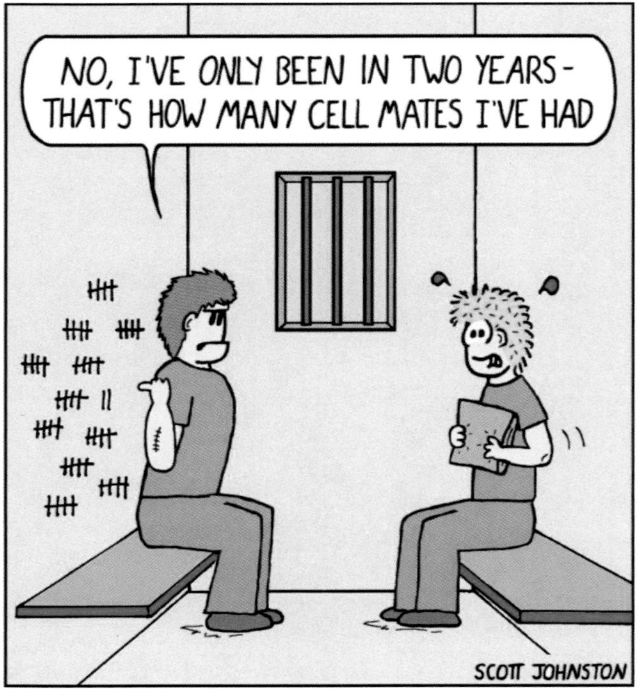
NO, I'VE ONLY BEEN IN TWO YEARS-
THAT'S HOW MANY CELL MATES I'VE HAD
SCOTT JOHNSTON

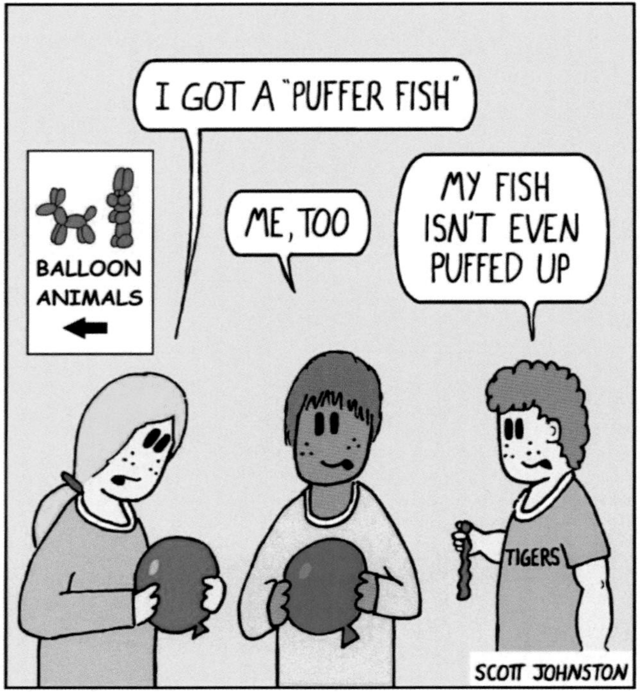
BALLOON ANIMALS
I GOT A "PUFFER FISH"
ME, TOO
MY FISH ISN'T EVEN PUFFED UP
TIGERS
SCOTT JOHNSTON

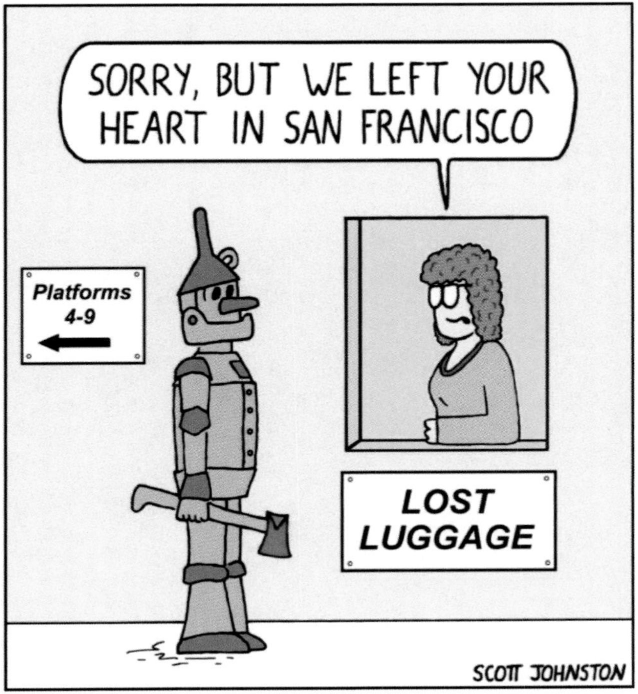
SORRY, BUT WE LEFT YOUR HEART IN SAN FRANCISCO
Platforms 4-9
LOST LUGGAGE
SCOTT JOHNSTON

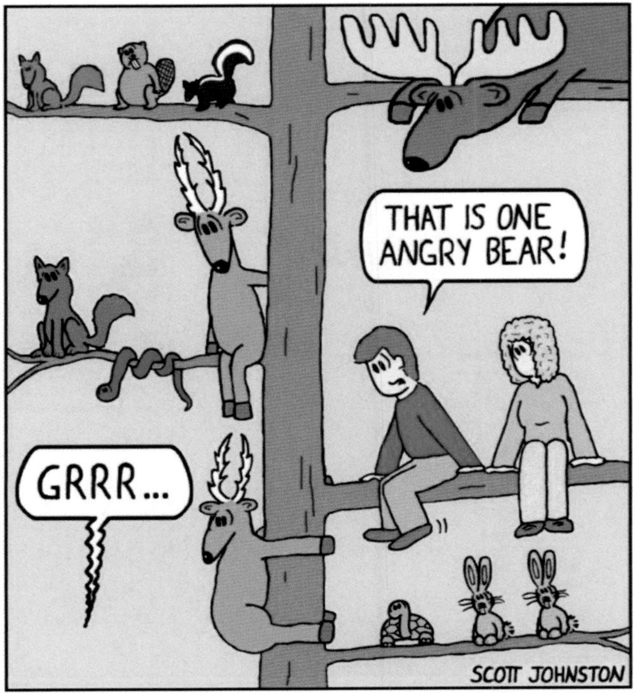
THAT IS ONE ANGRY BEAR!
GRRR...
SCOTT JOHNSTON

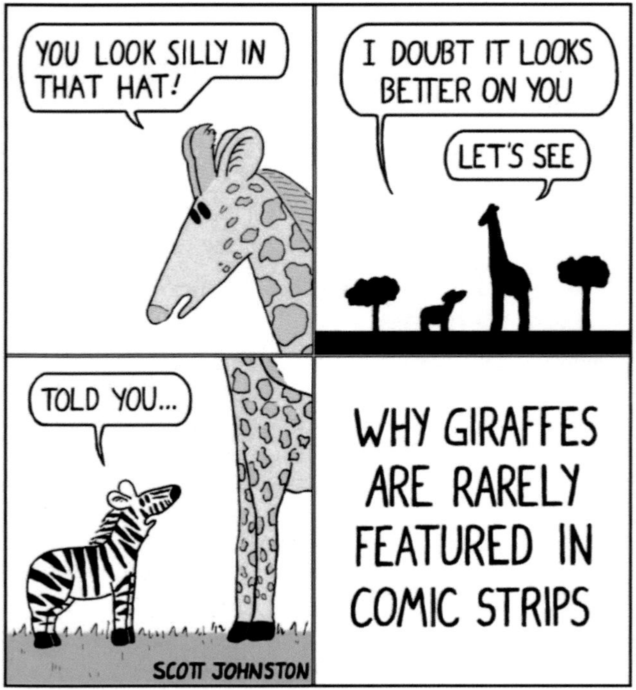
YOU LOOK SILLY IN THAT HAT!
I DOUBT IT LOOKS BETTER ON YOU
LET'S SEE
TOLD YOU...
WHY GIRAFFES ARE RARELY FEATURED IN COMIC STRIPS
SCOTT JOHNSTON

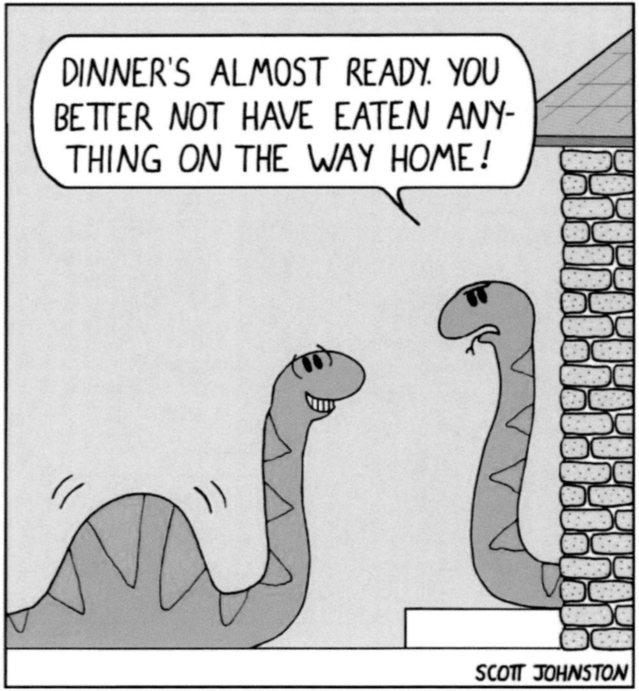
DINNER'S ALMOST READY. YOU BETTER NOT HAVE EATEN ANY-THING ON THE WAY HOME!
SCOTT JOHNSTON

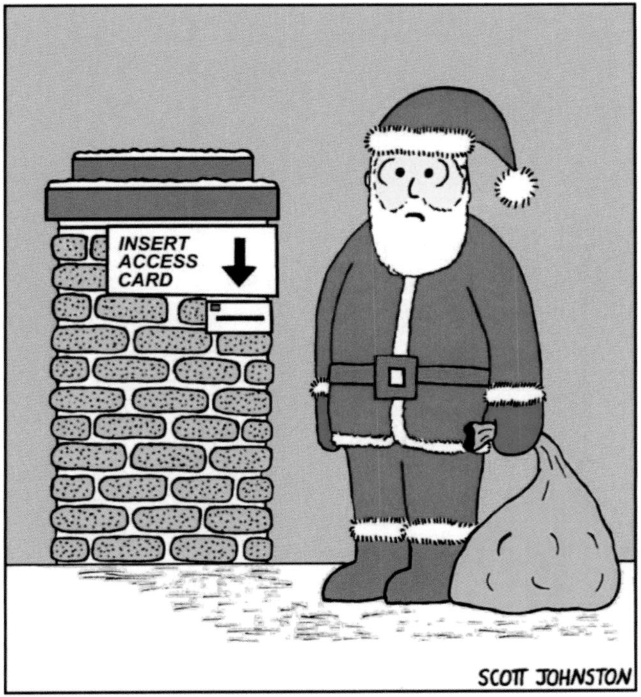
INSERT ACCESS CARD
SCOTT JOHNSTON

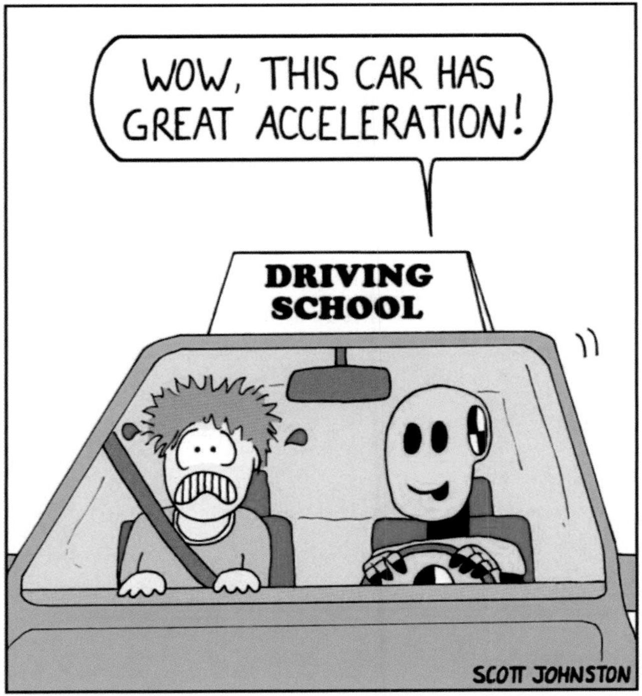
WOW, THIS CAR HAS GREAT ACCELERATION!
DRIVING SCHOOL
SCOTT JOHNSTON

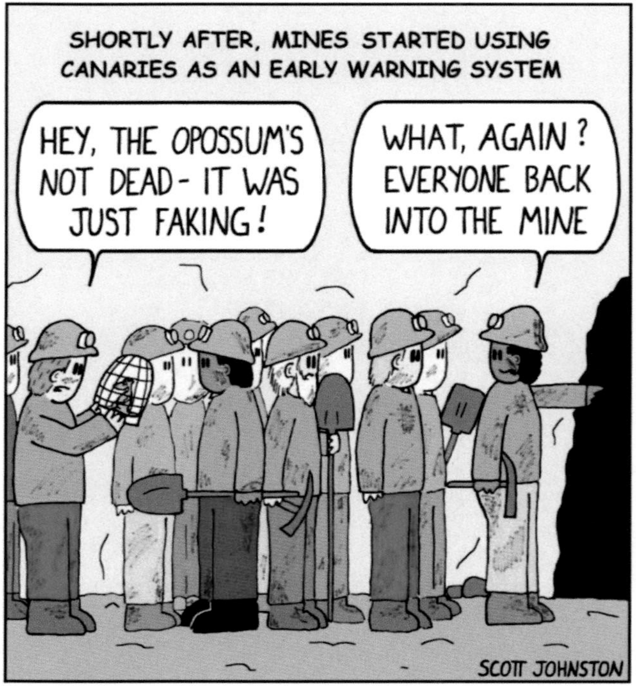
SHORTLY AFTER, MINES STARTED USING CANARIES AS AN EARLY WARNING SYSTEM
HEY, THE OPOSSUM'S NOT DEAD - IT WAS JUST FAKING!
WHAT, AGAIN? EVERYONE BACK INTO THE MINE
SCOTT JOHNSTON

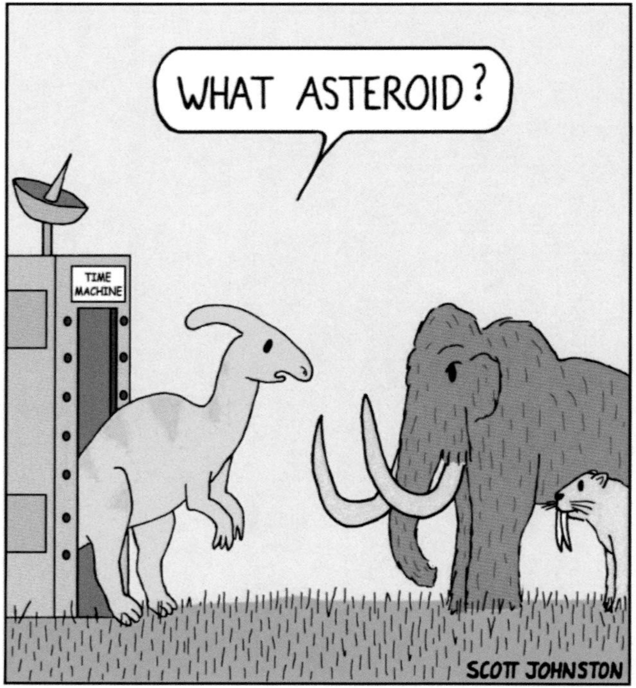
WHAT ASTEROID?
TIME MACHINE
SCOTT JOHNSTON

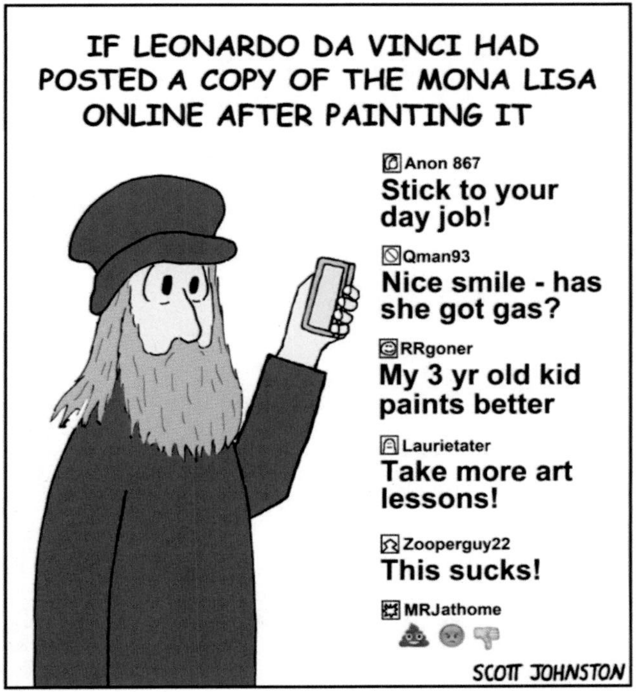
IF LEONARDO DA VINCI HAD POSTED A COPY OF THE MONA LISA ONLINE AFTER PAINTING IT
Anon 867
Stick to your day job!
Qman93
Nice smile - has she got gas?
RRgoner
My 3 yr old kid paints better
Laurietater
Take more art lessons!
Zooperguy22
This sucks!
MRJathome
SCOTT JOHNSTON

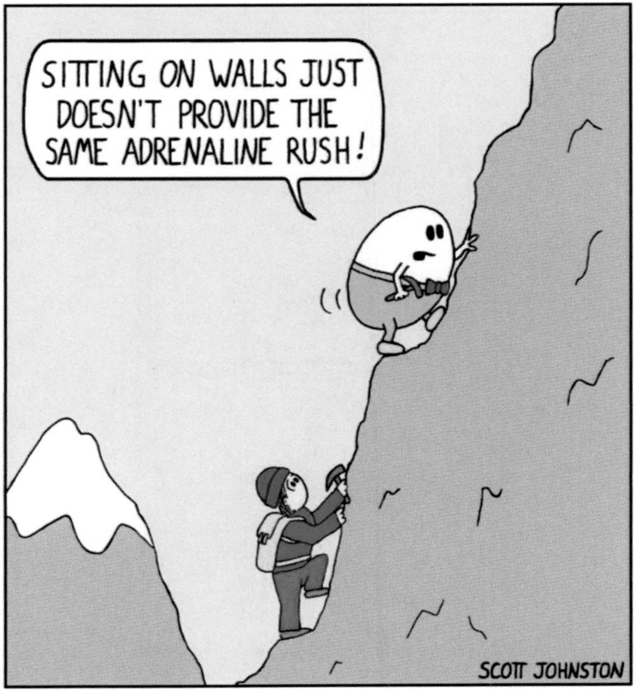
SITTING ON WALLS JUST DOESN'T PROVIDE THE SAME ADRENALINE RUSH!
SCOTT JOHNSTON

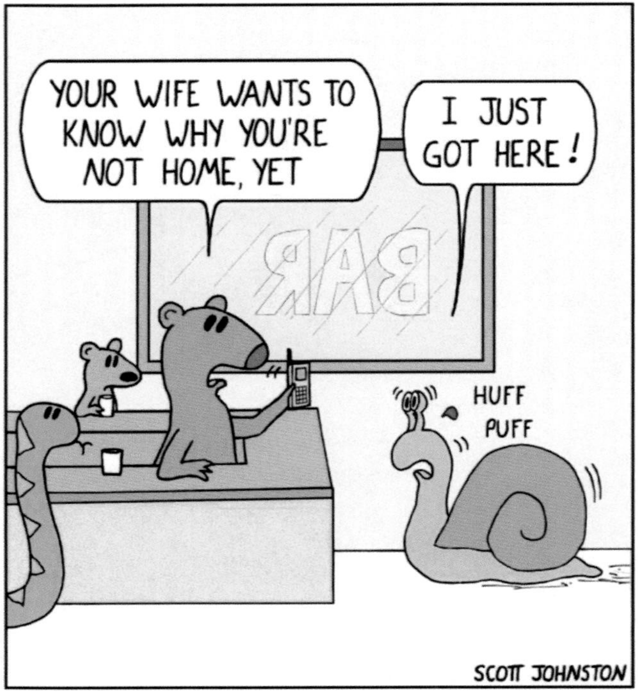
YOUR WIFE WANTS TO KNOW WHY YOU'RE NOT HOME, YET
I JUST GOT HERE!
BAR
HUFF
PUFF
SCOTT JOHNSTON

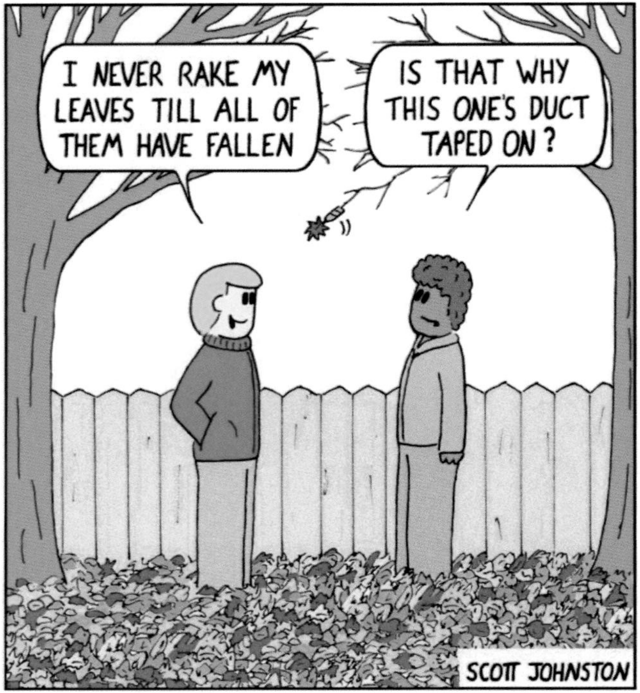
I NEVER RAKE MY LEAVES TILL ALL OF THEM HAVE FALLEN
IS THAT WHY THIS ONE'S DUCT TAPED ON?
SCOTT JOHNSTON

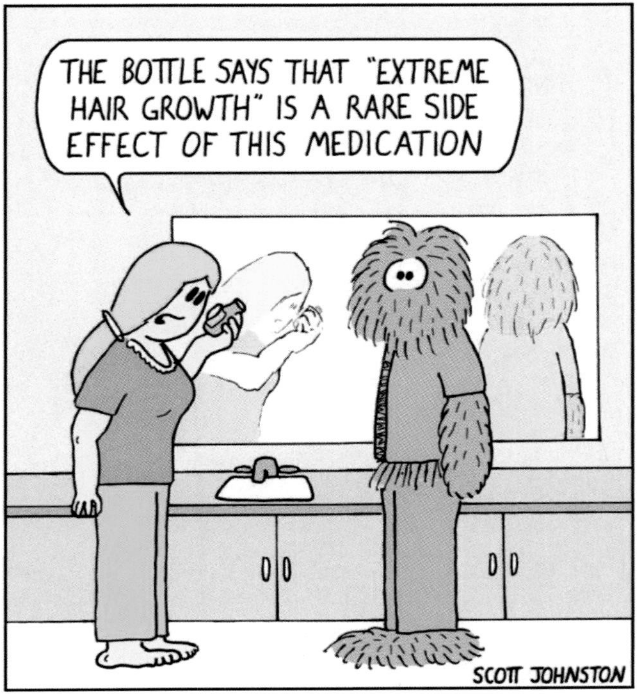
THE BOTTLE SAYS THAT "EXTREME HAIR GROWTH" IS A RARE SIDE EFFECT OF THIS MEDICATION
SCOTT JOHNSTON

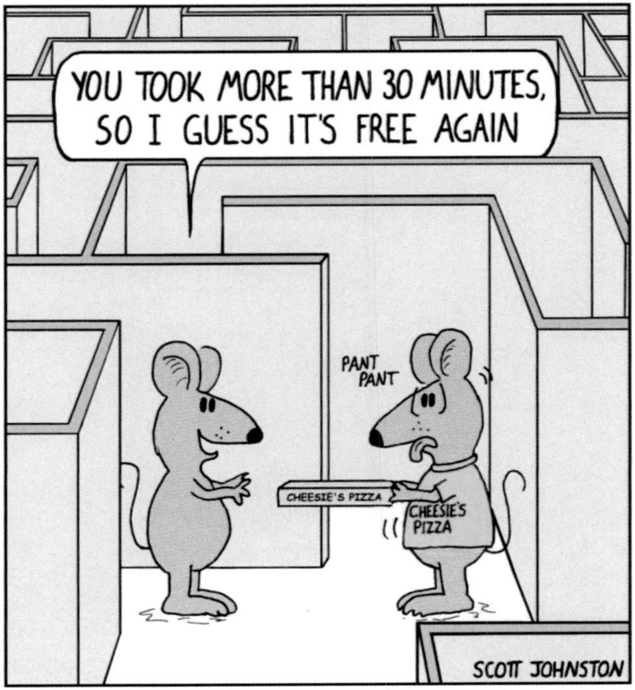
YOU TOOK MORE THAN 30 MINUTES, SO I GUESS IT'S FREE AGAIN
PANT PANT
CHEESIE'S PIZZA
CHEESIE'S PIZZA
SCOTT JOHNSTON

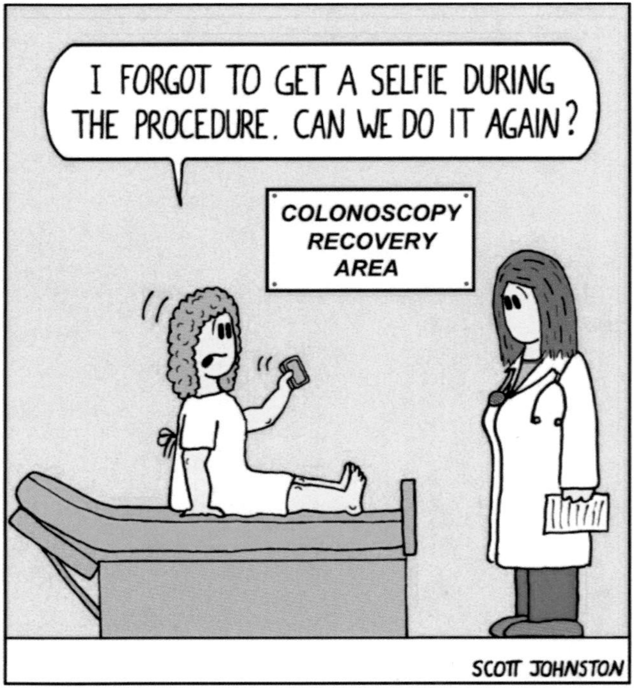
I FORGOT TO GET A SELFIE DURING THE PROCEDURE. CAN WE DO IT AGAIN?
COLONOSCOPY RECOVERY AREA
SCOTT JOHNSTON

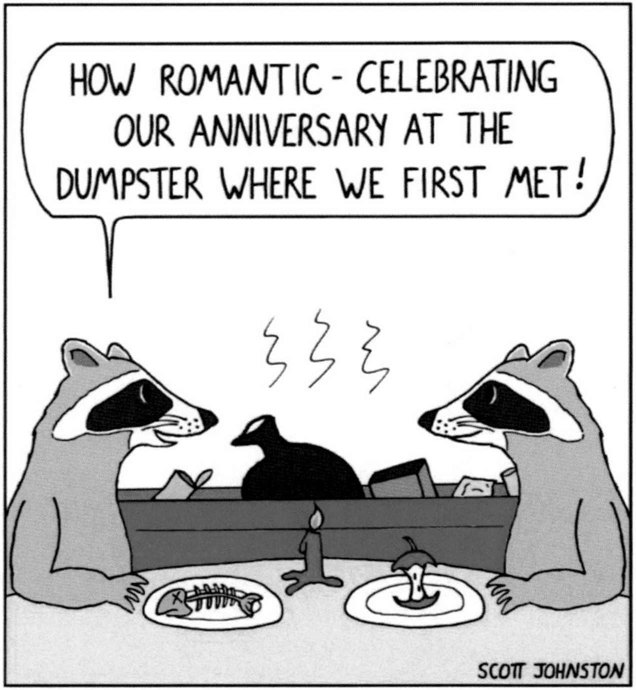
HOW ROMANTIC - CELEBRATING OUR ANNIVERSARY AT THE DUMPSTER WHERE WE FIRST MET!
SCOTT JOHNSTON

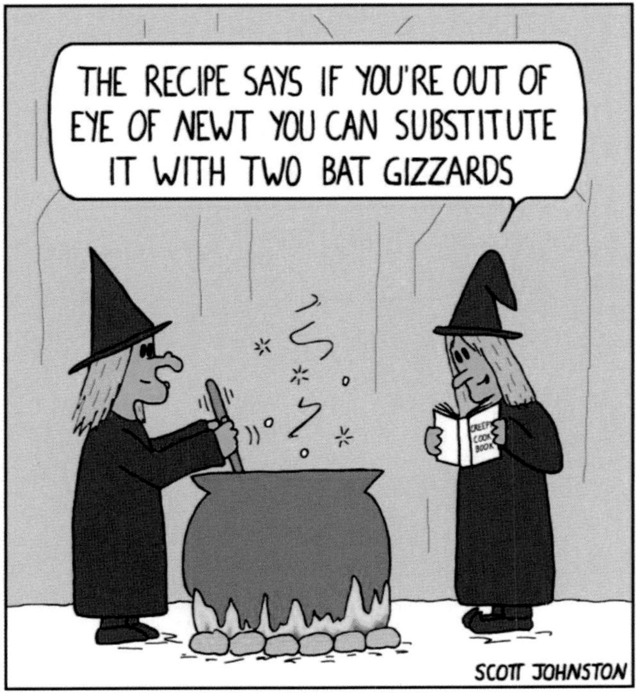
THE RECIPE SAYS IF YOU'RE OUT OF EYE OF NEWT YOU CAN SUBSTITUTE IT WITH TWO BAT GIZZARDS
CREEPY COOK BOOK
SCOTT JOHNSTON

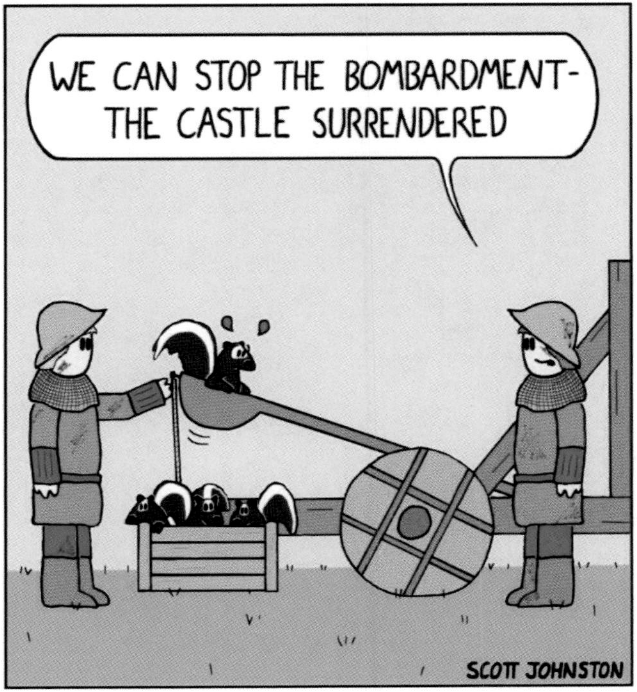
WE CAN STOP THE BOMBARDMENT- THE CASTLE SURRENDERED
SCOTT JOHNSTON

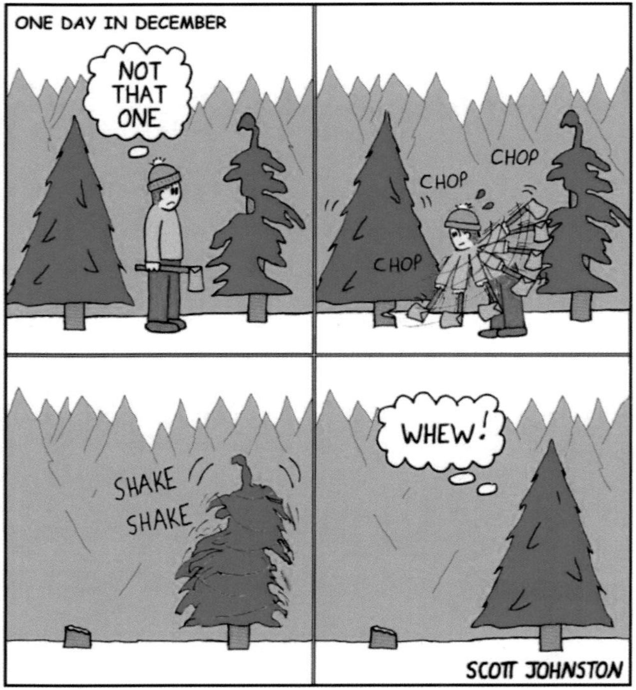
ONE DAY IN DECEMBER
NOT THAT ONE
CHOP
CHOP
CHOP
SHAKE
SHAKE
WHEW!
SCOTT JOHNSTON

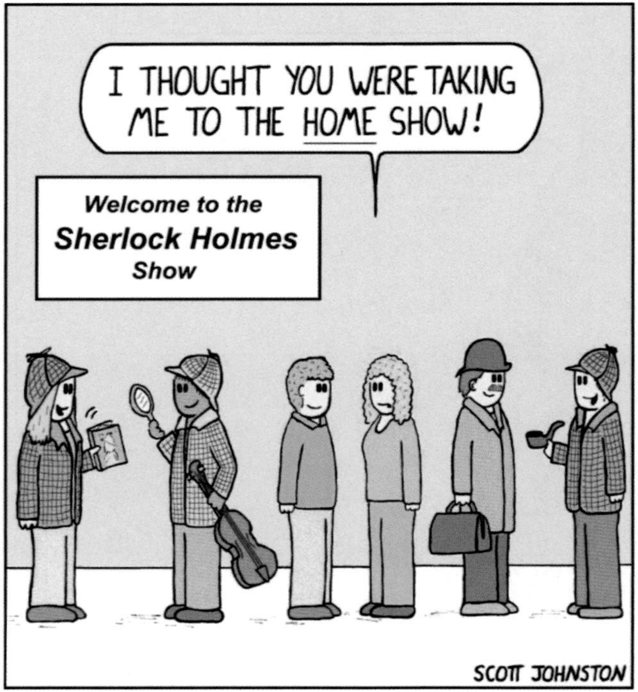
I THOUGHT YOU WERE TAKING ME TO THE HOME SHOW!
Welcome to the
Sherlock Holmes
Show
SCOTT JOHNSTON

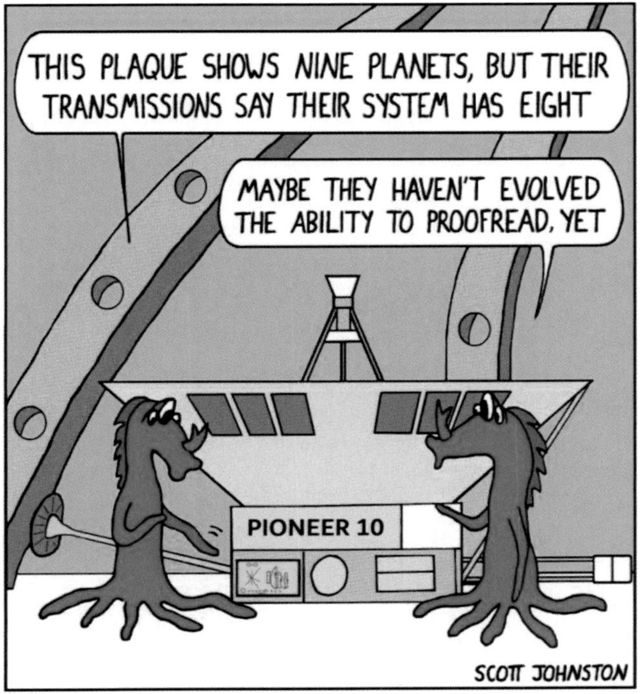
THIS PLAQUE SHOWS NINE PLANETS, BUT THEIR TRANSMISSIONS SAY THEIR SYSTEM HAS EIGHT
MAYBE THEY HAVEN'T EVOLVED THE ABILITY TO PROOFREAD, YET
PIONEER 10
SCOTT JOHNSTON

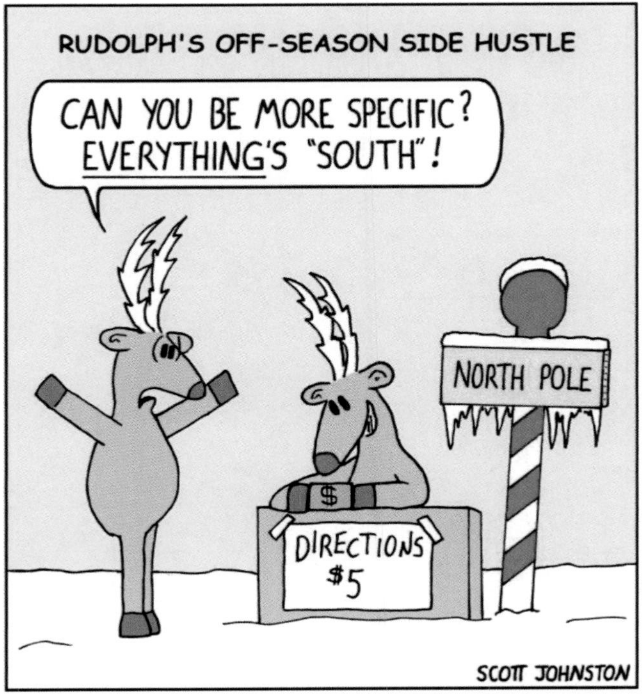
RUDOLPH'S OFF-SEASON SIDE HUSTLE
CAN YOU BE MORE SPECIFIC? EVERYTHING'S "SOUTH"!
NORTH POLE
$
DIRECTIONS $5
SCOTT JOHNSTON

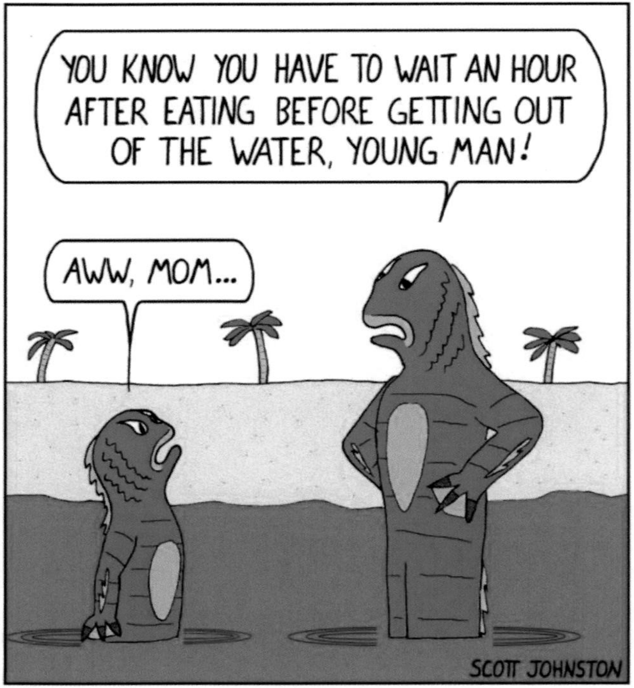
YOU KNOW YOU HAVE TO WAIT AN HOUR AFTER EATING BEFORE GETTING OUT OF THE WATER, YOUNG MAN!
AWW, MOM...
SCOTT JOHNSTON

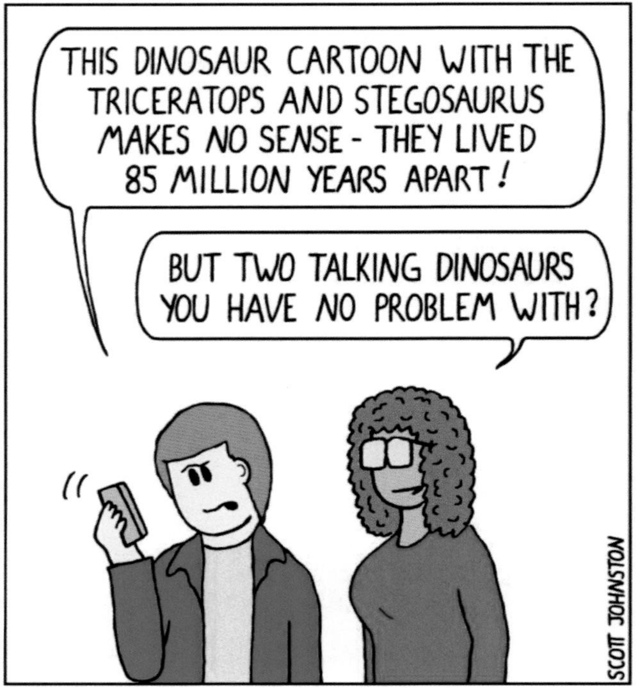
THIS DINOSAUR CARTOON WITH THE TRICERATOPS AND STEGOSAURUS MAKES NO SENSE - THEY LIVED 85 MILLION YEARS APART!
BUT TWO TALKING DINOSAURS YOU HAVE NO PROBLEM WITH?
SCOTT JOHNSTON

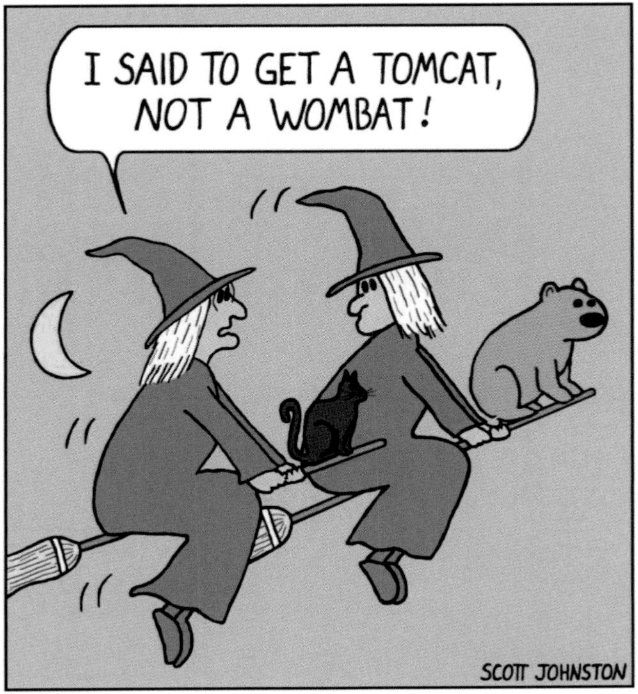
I SAID TO GET A TOMCAT, NOT A WOMBAT!
SCOTT JOHNSTON

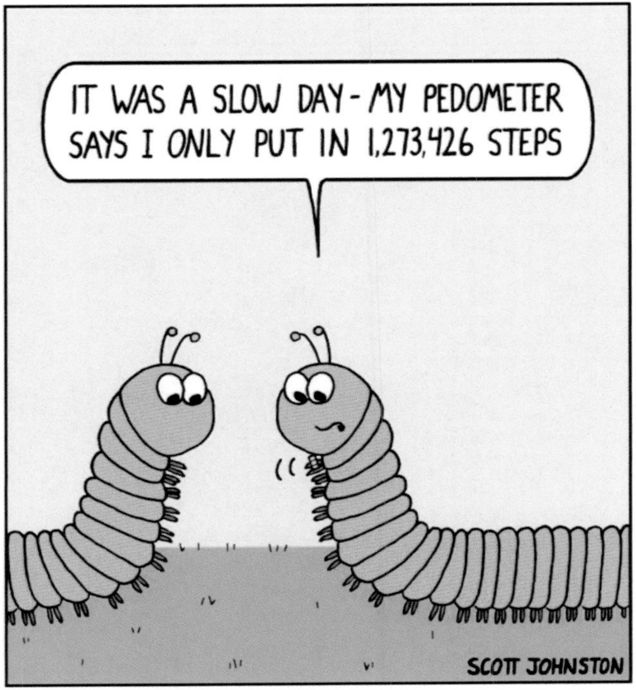
IT WAS A SLOW DAY - MY PEDOMETER SAYS I ONLY PUT IN 1,273,426 STEPS
SCOTT JOHNSTON

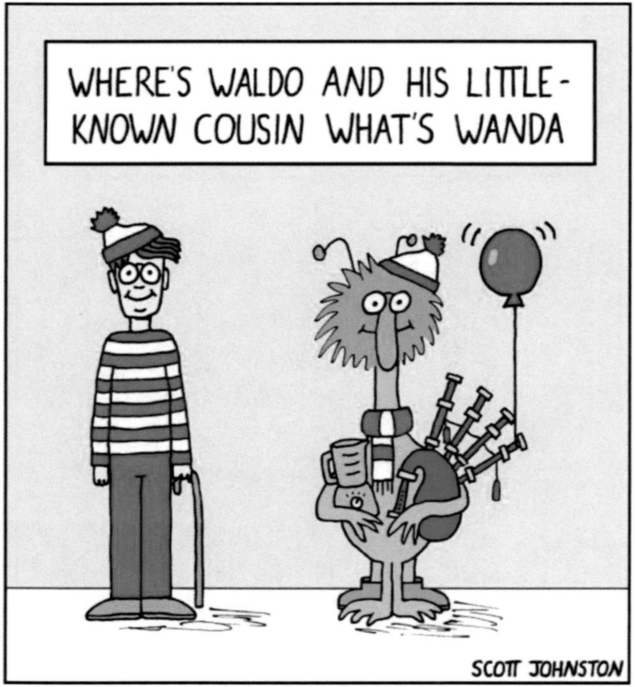
WHERE'S WALDO AND HIS LITTLE-KNOWN COUSIN WHAT'S WANDA
SCOTT JOHNSTON

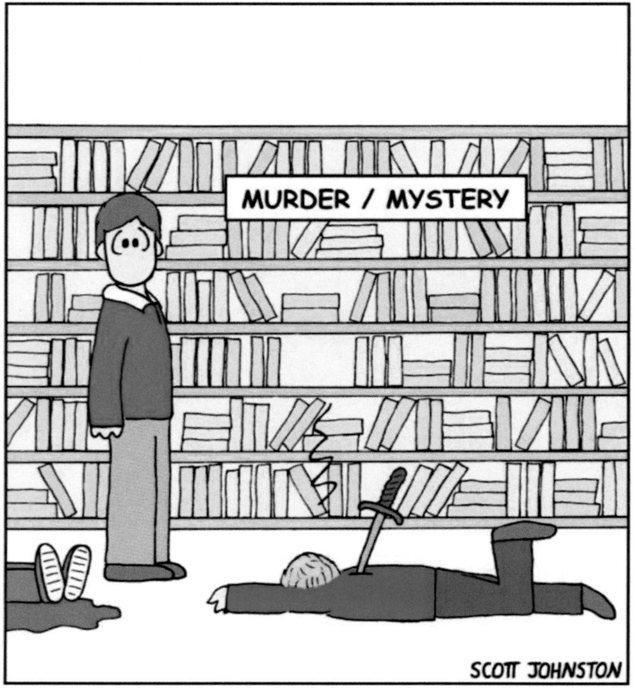
MURDER / MYSTERY
SCOTT JOHNSTON

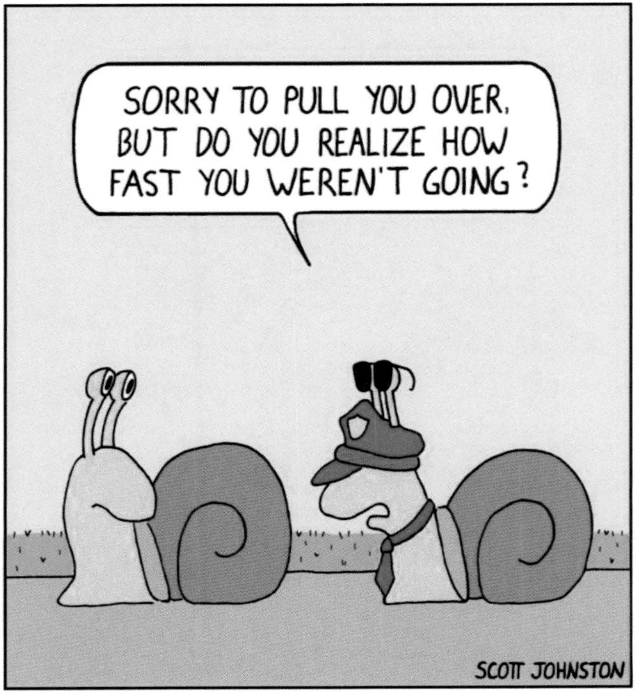
SORRY TO PULL YOU OVER, BUT DO YOU REALIZE HOW FAST YOU WEREN'T GOING?
SCOTT JOHNSTON

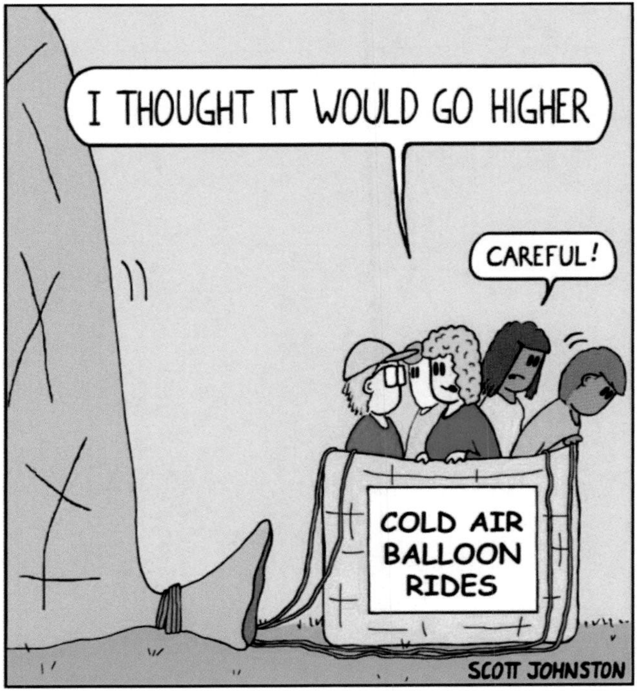
I THOUGHT IT WOULD GO HIGHER
CAREFUL!
COLD AIR BALLOON RIDES
SCOTT JOHNSTON

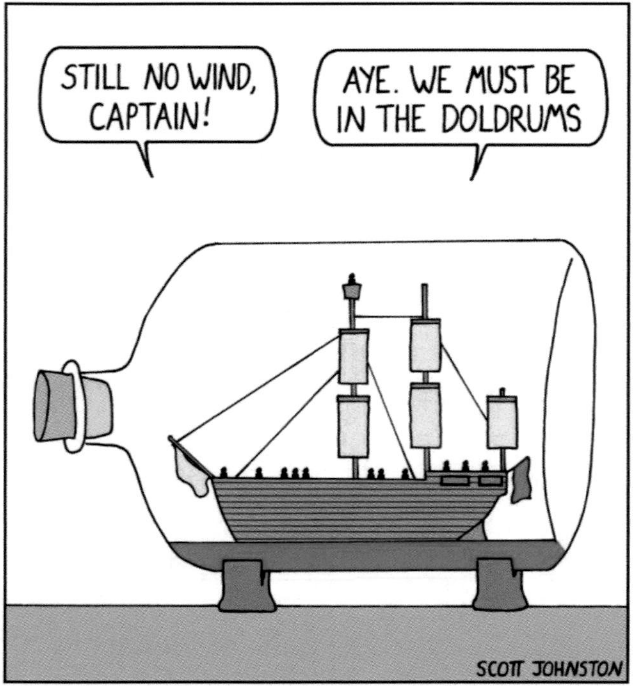
STILL NO WIND, CAPTAIN!
AYE. WE MUST BE IN THE DOLDRUMS
SCOTT JOHNSTON

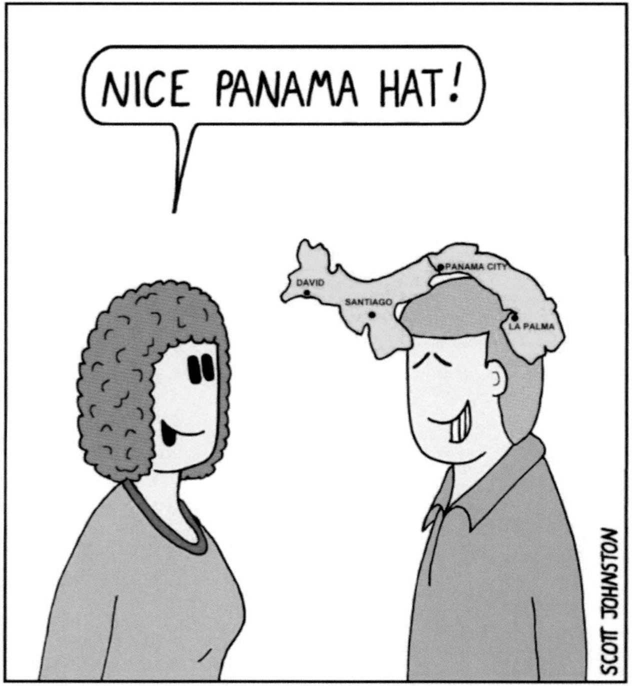
NICE PANAMA HAT!
DAVID
SANTIAGO
PANAMA CITY
LA PALMA
SCOTT JOHNSTON

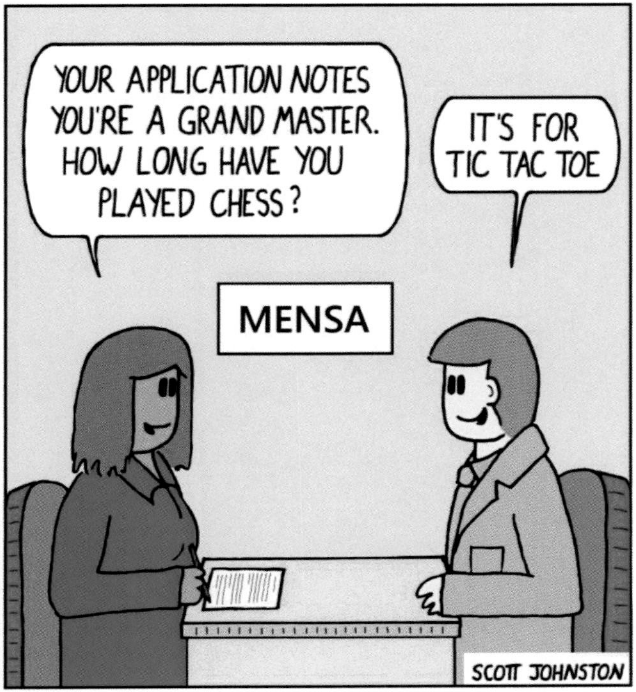
YOUR APPLICATION NOTES YOU'RE A GRAND MASTER. HOW LONG HAVE YOU PLAYED CHESS?
IT'S FOR TIC TAC TOE
MENSA
SCOTT JOHNSTON

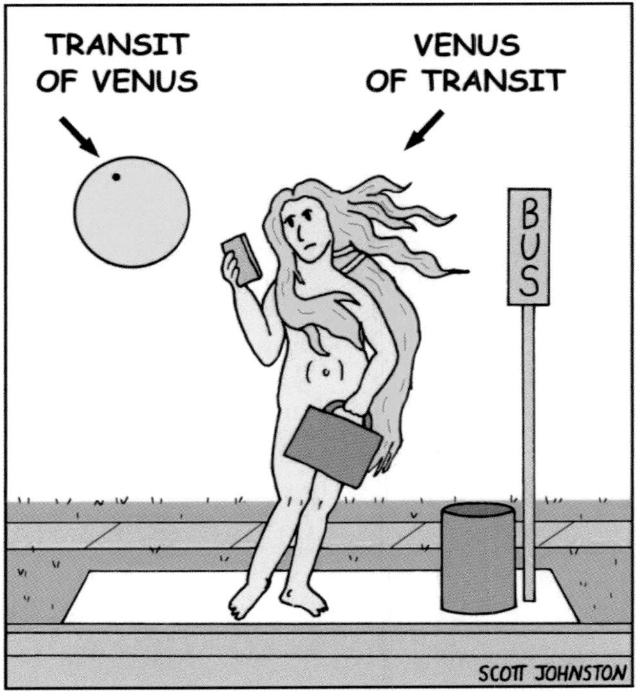
TRANSIT OF VENUS
VENUS OF TRANSIT
BUS
SCOTT JOHNSTON

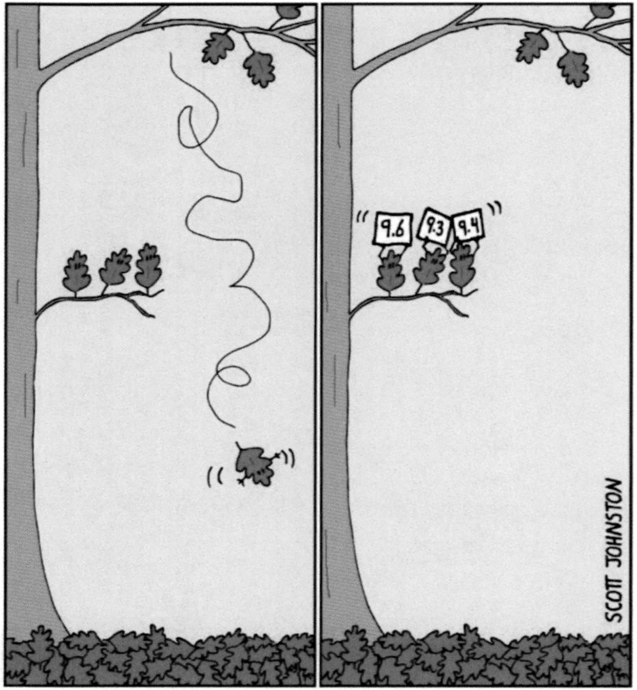
9.6
9.3
9.4
SCOTT JOHNSTON

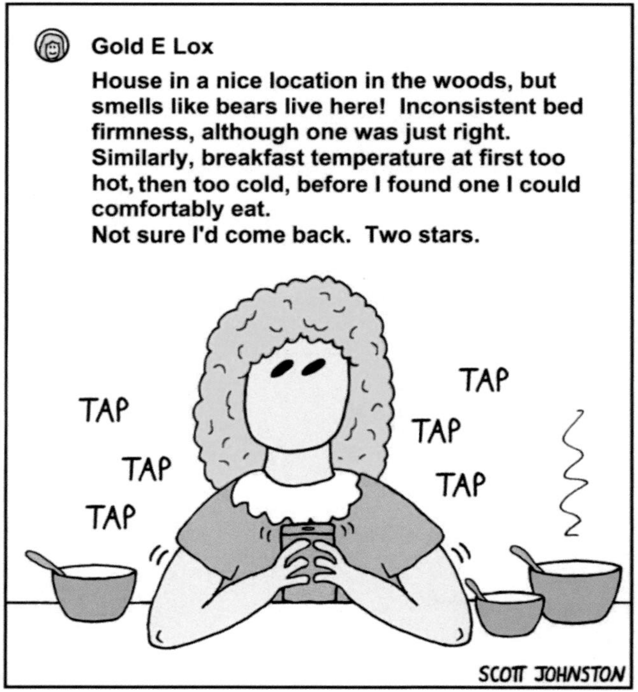
Gold E Lox
House in a nice location in the woods, but smells like bears live here! Inconsistent bed firmness, although one was just right. Similarly, breakfast temperature at first too hot, then too cold, before I found one I could comfortably eat.
Not sure I'd come back. Two stars.
TAP
TAP
TAP
TAP
TAP
TAP
SCOTT JOHNSTON

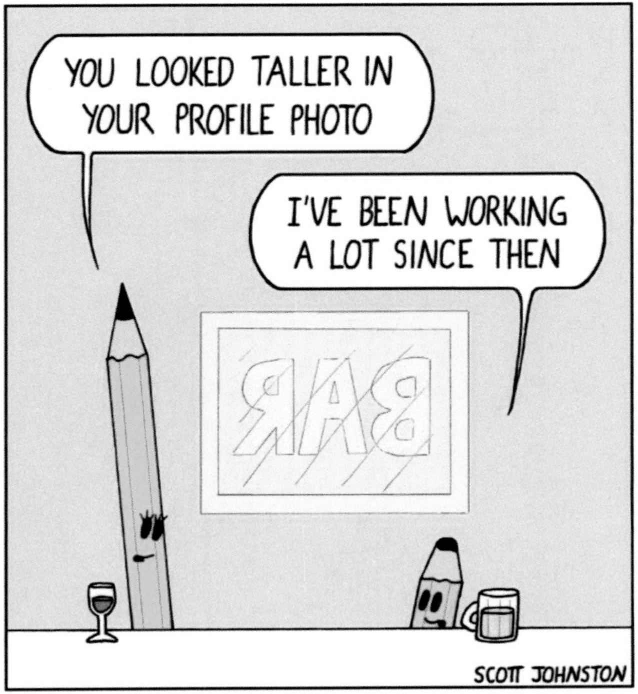
YOU LOOKED TALLER IN YOUR PROFILE PHOTO
I'VE BEEN WORKING A LOT SINCE THEN
SCOTT JOHNSTON

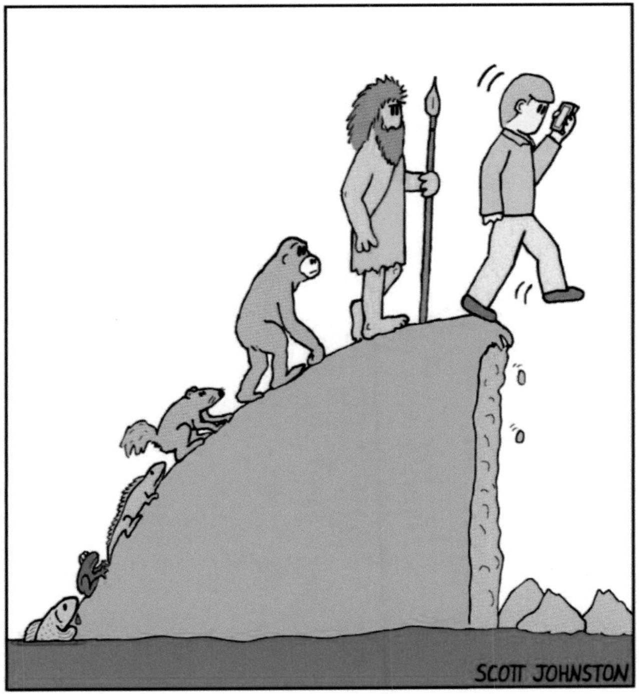
SCOTT JOHNSTON

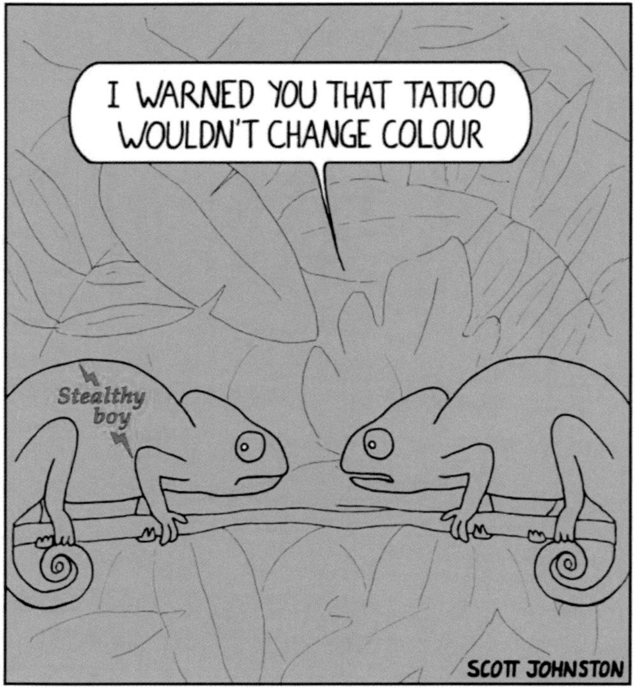
I WARNED YOU THAT TATTOO WOULDN'T CHANGE COLOUR
Stealthy boy
SCOTT JOHNSTON

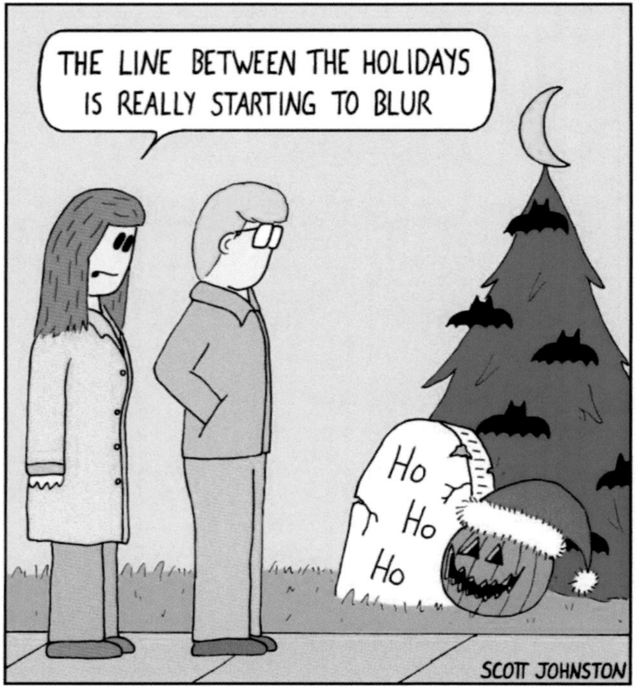
THE LINE BETWEEN THE HOLIDAYS IS REALLY STARTING TO BLUR
Ho
Ho
Ho
SCOTT JOHNSTON

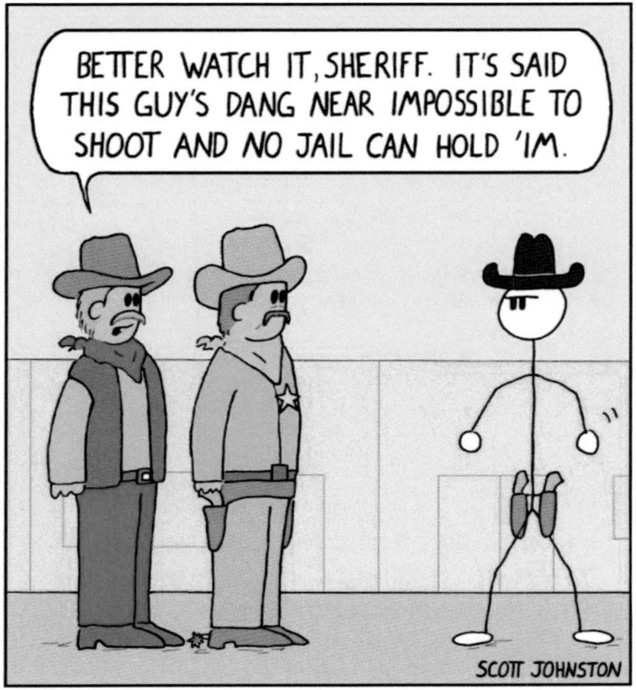
BETTER WATCH IT, SHERIFF. IT'S SAID THIS GUY'S DANG NEAR IMPOSSIBLE TO SHOOT AND NO JAIL CAN HOLD 'IM.
SCOTT JOHNSTON

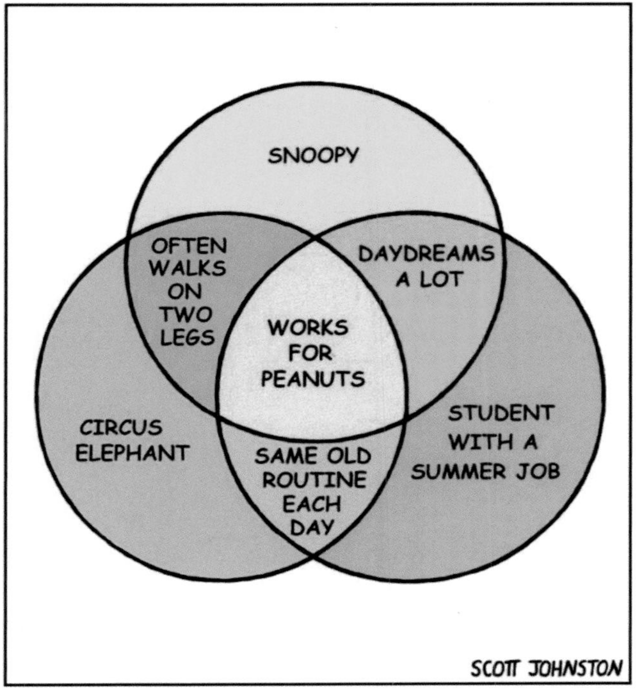
SNOOPY
OFTEN WALKS ON TWO LEGS
DAYDREAMS A LOT
WORKS FOR PEANUTS
CIRCUS ELEPHANT
SAME OLD ROUTINE EACH DAY
STUDENT WITH A SUMMER JOB
SCOTT JOHNSTON

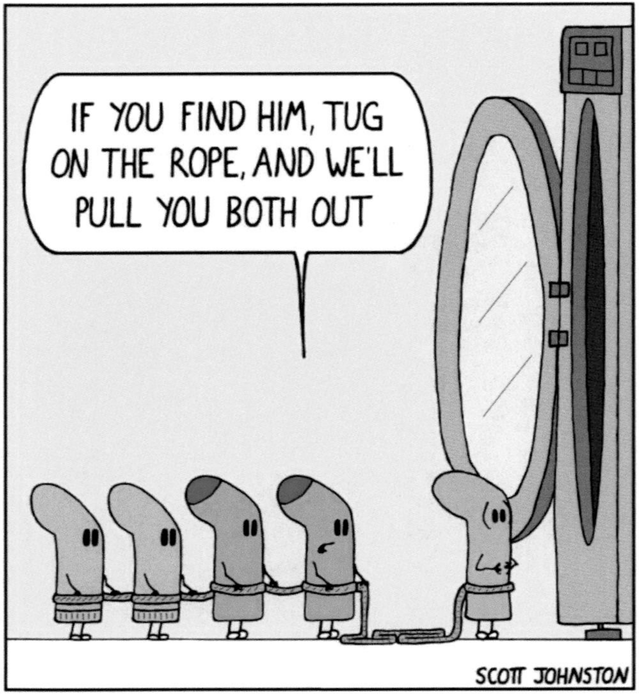
IF YOU FIND HIM, TUG ON THE ROPE, AND WE'LL PULL YOU BOTH OUT
SCOTT JOHNSTON

"Scott is like the folks that pave the road or deliver the potato chips to the corner store, you don't always see them, or know what they are up to, but what they do makes you feel better. Every community needs a determined cartoonist, like Scott. Someone who quietly carves out a spot for themself and importantly, make drawings that people feel are part of the world around them."

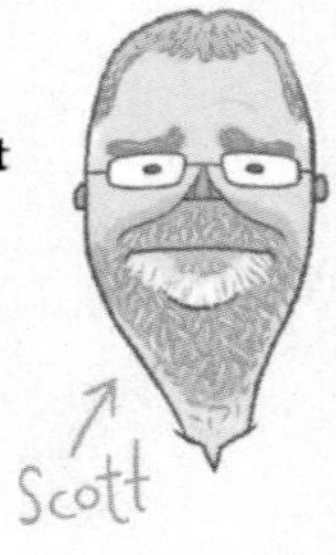
Scott

Wes Tyrell - ***President, Association of Canadian Cartoonists***

If you enjoyed this book and would like to see more of my cartoons, feel free to follow me at ScottJohnstonCartoons on Facebook, Instagram, or at www.ScottJohnstonCartoons.com

Manufactured by Amazon.ca
Bolton, ON

31991377R00057